TEST YOUR B*Q!

What's **Sinead**'s biggest fear?

What's **Edele**'s favorite movie?

What is **Lindsay** most proud of?

What kind of tattoo does **Keavy** have—and where?

FIND OUT ALL THE B*WITCHING ANSWERS IN

B*WITCHED

ST. MARTIN'S PAPERBACKS TITLES BY Anna Louise Golden

'N Sync

Five

Brandy

Backstreet Boys

The Moffatts

B*Witched

Anna Louise Golden

St. Martin's Paperbacks

> **NOTE:** If you purchased this book without a cover you should be aware that this book is stolen property. It was reported as "unsold and destroyed" to the publisher, and neither the author nor the publisher has received any payment for this "stripped book."

B*WITCHED

Copyright © 1999 by Anna Louise Golden
Cover photograph courtesy of ILPO MUSTO/London Features.

All rights reserved. No part of this book may be used or reproduced in any manner whatsoever without written permission except in the case of brief quotations embodied in critical articles or reviews. For information address St. Martin's Press, 175 Fifth Avenue, New York, N.Y. 10010.

ISBN: 0-312-97360-8

Printed in the United States of America

St. Martin's Paperbacks edition / August 1999

10 9 8 7 6 5 4 3 2 1

ACKNOWLEDGMENTS

THE PERSON I ALWAYS thank at the start of my acknowledgments is my agent, Madeleine Morel. It would be unthinkable to do anything less. The woman is amazing, on my side in everything, and to say "thank you" hardly fits the bill. My editor, Glenda Howard, is also remarkable. We've done a number of books together now, and she's simply a total joy to work with, particularly since she allowed herself to be convinced on this one!

Sharon Crisp, my researcher in England, did sterling work, fast and accurate. Kevan Roberts helped, too, for which I'm extremely grateful, particularly since he did it while on holiday. And then all the others who keep giving me encouragement: my Mum and Dad, assorted Leeds United supporters ... well, you know who you are. And always L&G.

The bottom line is that B*Witched are a great band, and great bands are hard to find, even in what's proving to be a golden age of pop. Certainly a lot of magazines reckon they're fab, which shows remarkably good taste, and more than a million fans can't be wrong. This book would have been harder without *Hit Sensations, Pop Star!, Teen Celebrity, Okej, KP, Big, Starlog Kissable Pinups, Exclusive!, 16, Smash Hits, dotmusic.com, E! Online, Tiger Beat,* and *Bop.*

Enjoy the music, have fun.

—ALG

Introduction

THEIR NAME MIGHT BE B*Witched, but you won't find any Samantha Stevens (or even Endora or Tabitha, for that matter) twitching her nose and performing magic. Just four Irish lasses casting a musical spell over you. In Britain, Australia, New Zealand, and all over Europe, they're massive. And now they've enthralled America. Right from the first note of their first single, "C'est La Vie," the country was captivated, making it into an immediate hit. And then, when their album, *B*Witched*, followed, it climbed straight up the charts, going platinum—over one million copies sold—in just *five* weeks. That's faster than the Spice Girls, Backstreet Boys, or 'N Sync managed. Call it another one for the girls.

Oh, just in case you hadn't already figured it out, these girls also like to wear denim. Lots of denim. They're a bunch of tomboys who can also be girlie girls, although it's not too often you're going to see any of them in a skirt or a dress—those jeans are just too comfortable for dancing, and they *love* to dance. If you saw their *In Concert* special on the Disney Channel (they shared the bill with the fab 5ive), or you've been lucky enough to have the chance to see them live, you'll know how much they like to move around on the stage. From start to finish, it's non-stop motion, and when they get to the section of Irish music in the middle of "C'est La Vie," it's like watching *Riverdance* without all the boring bits.

All along they've wanted an Irish element in their music, and insisted upon it. After all, they come from Dublin, and it's a part of who they are, and they're very proud of it. Yes, it helps set them apart, and having a whistle and a fiddle in your band (not to mention the Irish pipes on record!) adds a different and really cool element to the sound, but it's always going to be a case of "Does it work?" And with B*Witched it does.

Maybe that's because they co-write a lot of their material. You'll find plenty of bands who just perform other people's music, but these girls like to have a hand in everything—and why shouldn't they? It's nothing to do with Girl Power, that Spice Syndrome. It's just wanting to have more creative outlets.

And mentioning the Spices, B*Witched have managed something that the former never achieved. Edele, Keavy, Lindsay, and Sinead became the first female group *ever* to have their first four singles all enter the U.K. charts at Number One. Now that's not bad—and it's even more amazing when you consider that it happened within the space of twelve months! "C'est La Vie" hit first, just as it did in America, followed by "Rollercoaster," then the ballad "To You I Belong," a perfect hit for the Christmas season, and finally, in the spring of 1999, "Blame It on the Weatherman." Not a bad run. And who could forget the album. It didn't soar all the way to the top spot in Britain (just Number Three), but it still sold like the proverbial hotcakes.

That was only the tip of the iceberg. Add to that hits all over the world—they just love the girls in Australia and New Zealand among a zillion other places—and finally America. They've supported 'N Sync on tour, about as sweet a gig as you're going to find anywhere, and gone out on the road with 98 Degrees. Does life get any better than that?

Well, yes. It gets better when you have a hit single and a major hit album, which is exactly what they've achieved in the U.S. Still, nothing could compare with that first British Number One!

"It was amazing," Keavy said. "We'd imagined lots of things would happen—like getting a record deal and going into a studio—but never going straight in the charts at Number One like that! When it finally sank in, there was a bit of excitement, I can tell you."

Once it all sank in that it was real, you could say the girls were happy. But, in spite of all the hits, and the tours and the fame, they insist, "We're more interested in bringing joy into people's lives than becoming incredibly famous."

Of course, this is what they all always wanted to do. From the first time they got together at Digges Lane Dance Centre in Dublin, Ireland, it was apparent that they had something special together, some chemistry that clicked. Edele, Sinead, and Keavy all had full-time jobs, while Lindsay was still at school. And so they met up every evening, working out routines and songs.

It didn't hurt that two of the girls already knew a bonafide star—Shane of Boyzone, who have been one of the top boy bands in the U.K. for several years, a group now trying to break through in America. How well did they known him? Well, Edele and Keavy had literally grown up with him—he is their brother. So they had the inspiration, and knew that good things could happen. All you needed was a lucky break.

Of course, some breaks are luckier than others—and some come faster. Were the girls ready for their first public performance—on Irish national television!—three weeks later? Not really, but they did it anyway, and went over as if the world, or at least the country, had been waiting for them. And maybe it had.

One thing led to another. They were asked to open for Boyzone on their Irish tour (and no, family connections had nothing to do with it—this was all about talent). Once again, they were the bomb.

Meanwhile, they'd hooked up with the people who would become their managers, Kim Glover and Tommy J. Smith, who worked with producer Ray Hedges. This was the new "family" for the lasses.

There was only so far you could go in Ireland as a band. If you wanted to kick it big, there was only one place to do it, and that was London. So that was where the girls went. Going through a number of band names (they started off as D'Zire, then Sassy, and Sister, finally settling on B*Witched, which just seemed to have the right . . . magic). It was actually Ray Hedges's idea to call them that, according to Edele.

"Our producer came up with it when our managers told him about [our] girl band, and he said, 'No, I'm not working with girls.' He didn't want to work with us, then we met him and he said we just 'bewitched' him." So why the * in there? Well, it's a little bit more sparkly, just like the lasses themselves, and while it's pronounced *bewitched*, it avoids any kind of confusion with the Sixties television sitcom that starred the late (and lovely) Elizabeth Montgomery as a witch living a suburban life.

Certainly the name seemed to put a spell on people. Before they knew what was happening, they had a development deal with Epic, which gave them nine months to come up with some songs. In the course of just a few weeks they'd written "C'est La Vie" and "To You I Belong." It was hard work, but it paid off—Epic loved what they were hearing and decided to release their record.

To prepare, they hit the road opening for 911, one of a wave of new Brit boy bands, then filmed a video for what would be the first single—"C'est La Vie."

And from that point on, it was all madness. Everyone wanted to know them. They were on television, in the press. You name it, they did it. And it just got even more mental when the single started appearing all over Europe and hitting the charts in Germany, France, and Sweden. Then "Rollercoaster" followed its predecessor all the way to the top spot, and the girls couldn't have been more famous if they'd been royalty.

In their denim and trainers, they dressed like a million girls in the street, but with an edge. They were people everyone could relate to, down to earth, and very tomboyish. "We've been named the first tomboy band ever," laughed Lindsay. And it wasn't just an act. Keavy's first job had been as an apprentice mechanic at her dad's garage, while she and Lindsay both trained as kickboxers—not the girliest things in the world. While they loved to shop, denim was really what they wore.

"Onstage, we always wear denim, and when we get off stage we still wear denim," said Keavy. "If we're at a fancier show, we wear denim with sequins on it."

Their album, *B*Witched*, appeared in Britain in the fall of 1998, and took everyone by surprise. Those who thought they knew them from their two hits were stunned by the range of music the record contained. But that was part of the plan.

"When we first started to write," explained Keavy, "we never wanted B*Witched to be about one thing, about one style of music, so we've got all different kinds."

And it was true. There was pure pop, some hip-hop, even some indie and alternative. Something for everyone—and it seemed as if everyone rushed out and bought it, because the album went straight into the British chart at Number Three. That was a cause for celebration, if ever there was one. One hit single could have been a fluke. Even two could have been nothing more than good luck. But a major album . . . well, that was something else, when albums in the U.K. cost around $20; not exactly an impulse purchase.

The year 1998 was rapidly becoming one for all the girls to remember, but the whirlwind was about to gather them up and carry them off, quite literally. There were lightning trips to Australia, Japan, and America, where companies were suddenly *very* interested in releasing their records, before heading home—well, to England, anyway, their home away from home—to prepare for the release of their third single, "To You I Belong," as well as a performance on the *Royal Variety Show*, where they all got to meet Prince Charles. And in between all that, there were more trips, back to Australia and Japan, then Europe, as well as the

MTV Europe Awards in lovely Rome, where they sang "Rollercoaster."

But maybe the biggest thrill was when "To You I Belong" became their third single to hit Number One, right before Christmas, probably the best present any of the girls could have asked for. They even managed to have a great laugh when taping the Christmas edition of *Top of the Pops* (a British chart TV show). Since Edele and Keavy are identical twins, they decided to swap outfits, and do their hair in each other's style. Not only did they manage to fool the audience, they also fooled Lindsay and Sinead!

It had been a great year, and they deserved some time off. But it wasn't going to be much. A few days in Dublin visiting parents and friends was all they could manage. Why? Because, as the clocks ticked over into 1999, they were about to go on the road again. And this time it would be in America. Even though they didn't have a record out yet, they were supporting 'N Sync on their U.S. tour—and that meant playing to massive crowds of screaming fans. What better introduction to the country?

"We do loads of traveling and it's definitely the highlight for me," Sinead said. "There's nothing better than loving what you do and getting to fly all over the world. We're so lucky!"

Going around the country on their own twelve-seater bus was a new experience, as was the idea of playing in big shopping malls. But it let American audiences know who they were. Since they spent two and a half months in the U.S., they obviously became very familiar with it, even managing a trip to Disneyland. And that certainly paid off—once "C'est La Vie" was released in the States, it was immediately chart-bound, selling over half a million copies and going gold! With a great sense of timing, the record appeared right before St. Patrick's Day (how very Irish!)

"The record company planned it," said Keavy, "when the promotions would start, and they picked that day."

That was impressive enough, but it paled in performance to the album. Hitting the stores in April, it crashed into the Top Twenty, going all the way to Number Twelve, and turning platinum (over one million copies sold) in just five weeks—that's faster than the Spice Girls or any of the boy bands had managed with their debuts. If you wanted an indication of what America thought of B*Witched, that was your answer—and it was obviously something very, very good.

Of course, people have called them Ireland's answer to the Spice Girls, because they're female and sing. But nothing could be further from the truth. The Spices might have paved the way, but B*Witched aren't about Girl Power (they admire it, but for them this is all about music, not politics); they're about music and having a good time. "Our message is more about living life to the full," they say, and "going for your dreams because you only live once."

And they've certainly proved that going for those dreams can work, and in a major way. They spent half of 1998 pinching themselves, trying to believe it was all real, and now they're working their butts off. There's just no rest for them. After the fourth U.K. Number One single, "Blame It on the Weatherman," it was back to America, taping the Disney *In Concert* special, then back to England to work on their next album.

With that almost complete, it was back across the Atlantic again (and you have to hope they're keeping track of all those air miles!) to start another long tour of North America, in the company of 98 Degrees—and very good company that is, indeed.

If, as they've said, "Rollercoaster" was written to describe how they felt about their first year together, you have to wonder what songs will come out of 1999 . . . somehow "Bus Trip" doesn't sound anywhere near as good, does it?

Once they've seen America yet again—and you just know there's going to be another single or two coming this-summer, although whether it'll be the same as the British singles remains to be seen—there'll be a brand-new single, from the upcoming album, out in other parts of the world, so they'll be dashing around to promote that. The album, which is still untitled, is set for a fall release in the U.K., to be followed by a tour. You could probably call B*Witched the hardest-working girls in show business and be very close to the truth. In fact, as Sinead said, the reality is, "we're in love with our job."

Very few bands have had as much success as quickly as B*Witched. To have gone from nothing to winning over the world in a year is a staggering feat. Obviously, it's more than luck, and it's more than marketing. Luck will carry you so far. So will marketing. To get the rest of the way, you need what these four girls have—talent. A lot of enthusiasm helps, too. Or maybe they really do have more than a touch of magic about them. . . .

PART ONE

The Girls

Dublin

*I*T'S HARDLY A SECRET that any band is a mix of people, and for it to work, the chemistry has to be just right. Sometimes that happens, everything clicks, and things take off in a way no one could have imagined. Sometimes it doesn't, and five years later you're no further along than when you started, with nothing but a dream and a lot of work to show for what you'd hoped. The incredible rise of B*Witched means that they obviously have the formula perfect. Four girls who've come together in the right time and place, who meld together as if they were one.

But they're not one, of course. They're four strong individuals. Even Edele and Keavy, the twins, are very different from each other, and that's just the way it should be. They all bring different things, different experiences, influences and backgrounds to the group. The one thing they have in common is Dublin.

The capital city of Ireland is a beautiful place. O'Connell Street is the equal of any lovely avenue anywhere in the world. There's a romance about the city that brings out the dreamer in people. No wonder it's been home to a lot of great artists in many fields. James Joyce, the famous writer, set most of his work in Dublin. U2, who've become one of the biggest rock bands in the world, hail from there. Writer Roddy Doyle, author of *The Commitments*, *The Van*, and *The Snapper*, among other books—and all three have been successful films—is a Dublin man. It's a place alive with words and music, home to a great university and theater. In Dublin, as in the rest of Ireland, people love to talk. Even when times are hard, they seem to be happy. Music leaps out of places. Even the smallest of bars—the social centers of Ireland—has music, people sitting down and playing together in what they call sessions, messing around with the old tunes, so that even if you don't know them, you somehow take in the traditional music by a kind of osmosis.

Ireland is justifiably proud of its history and culture. A thousand years ago, Dublin was the Viking capital of the country, after the Norsemen had come over from Scandinavia. Before that there was the rule of the legendary Irish kings. Later there would be oppression by the English, and in the great potato famine—potatoes had been the staple diet of the Irish farm laborers—many left for America, and many died.

That was then, however, and this is now. Ireland's international image might be built on its beautiful countryside and charming little villages (think *Ballykissangel* on PBS), but the reality is that Ireland's as much a modern country as anywhere else. Dublin is a major cosmopolitan city these days, as wired and high-tech as any place you can name. And in people like U2, the Cranberries, Boyzone, and now B*Witched, they have a strong musical representation on the global scene, too.

That's the Dublin where the girls grew up (apart from Lindsay, but more about her later). It's what they know. They might all speak with a strong Irish brogue, but don't let it fool you into thinking they're a bunch of hicks—quite the opposite is true. Down to earth, yes, and completely without pretension. But they're all city girls. If you took them to a farm and asked them to milk a cow, they wouldn't have a clue what to do!

Still, that's quite all right. One of the things about being a pop star is that you never need to know how to milk a cow or do a lot of other things—as long as you can entertain. And B*Witched more than succeed in that department.

So they've got the chemistry, they've got the songs, they've got the moves—they've got it all. But who exactly are they? What makes Sinead, Keavy, Edele, and Lindsay tick? What makes them exactly who they are? The best way to find out is by taking a look at each of them, and finding out more about them. . . .

Sinead

At twenty-one, Sinead is the oldest member of the band. Sinead Maria O'Carroll, as she was christened, was born in Dublin on May 14, 1978. Before she had any idea what was happening, though, her parents moved a little way outside the city, to Newbridge in County Kildare. It wasn't really that far from the city, just far enough to feel removed and comfortable, away from the rush and the crowds, which was exactly what Eamonn and Barbara O'Carroll wanted for their new baby girl.

Eamonn had apprenticed as an electrician and had his own company; it was hard work, but paid well. When the family settled in Newbridge, Barbara, ambitious herself, opened a shop selling lingerie. It made for a busy life, especially as more children came along to join Sinead. First there was Elaine, then Ailish, and finally a boy, Paul, to complete the family.

It was a good life in Newbridge, a fine place to be a kid, where you could go off exploring in the countryside in fine weather. And the O'Carrolls loved the countryside. Sometimes they'd all get in the car and take off, exploring various bits of Ireland. In fact, Sinead's first memory is from one of those trips, out to a place called the Ring of Kerry. What had started as sunshine turned to fog as they neared the ring, getting even thicker as they climbed the hill on which it was situated. At the top, clear even in the fog,

Sinead saw a stone cross, and wondered if somehow, after the long climb, she'd reached heaven!

When she was four years old. Sinead's parents enrolled her in dance class. It was immediately apparent that she had definite talent as a dancer. In fact, for seven years, from the ages of eight to fifteen, she took classes in Irish dancing, taught by a woman named Mary Donaghue—if she'd stuck with it she might even have ended up as part of *Riverdance*! She loved Irish dancing, but never thought it was something she'd use in her life, let alone in her music. But there she was, during the Irish jig break on "C'est La vie," step dancing like she'd been born to it—and in fact she helped the others learn what to do.

"If anyone told me I'd be Irish dancing to a pop song when I was older, I'd have thought they were absolutely mad!" she laughed. "But it suited the song and people seemed to like it. We had a lot of fun messing around, but that's it—don't expect B*Witched to make a habit of entertaining you like that!"

Like any good Catholic girl, her first Holy Communion was a high point in young Sinead's life, undertaken when she was seven years old. She was having hers alongside her best friend, Suzanne Hennessy. Naturally, the whole family was there for the occasion, which, with parties and everything else, was a daylong affair. Sinead had a special new dress for the event, and everything was white. It was a short dress, coming just to her knees, with plenty of petticoats underneath, worn with white knee socks and new white shoes, as well as a white veil and white parasol to keep off the sun. The clothes were already laid out on her bed when she awoke that morning, and even getting dressed seemed to take on the feeling of a ritual. Once she was dressed and looked at herself in the mirror, she thought she looked just like a princess from a fairy tale. Her biggest memory of the day, though, was that almost every minute it seemed as if someone wanted to take a photograph of her.

Music was always an important part of her life, and one of her favorite subjects at school, where she learned to play the piano a little. The first record she ever bought was "Fame" by Irene Cara, the theme from the movie of the same name. The movie had come out in 1980, when Sinead was only two, and of course she didn't remember it then! But she saw it later, and it was a great inspiration to her as a dancer to see kids moving around like that. So when the record was re-released, a few years later, she pounced on it for the start of her collection!

Her other favorite subject at school was French, probably because she happened to be very good at it. In fact, in her teens, Sinead would spend some time in France and actually become quite fluent in the language, although she's forgotten some of that now—who wouldn't, with so much on her mind?

Although she did well at school, always making good grades in her work, there was also another side to her. Being small, she tried to make up for her size by being loud, which didn't always sit too well with the teachers. What sat even worse was when Sinead, angry about something that had happened, came in and threw eggs all over the other students in her class. That was something that couldn't be ignored, and she was off to see the headmistress.

"It was the naughtiest thing I've ever done and I got suspended," she admitted. "But it was worth it!"

She did come back from it, however, to be named Schoolgirl of the Year at her school in her "transition year," as they call it in Ireland (under the system there, the transition year is the year between elementary and secondary school), which was no small achievement. And in spite of being small, she was a good athlete, even if she didn't think she was—she won medals one year in the hurdles, gymnastics, and sprint competitions, which she still has.

Outside of her schoolwork, however, it was dancing that really captured her imagination and her time. Not only did she study Irish dancing, but she also competed in it. Her teacher, Mary Donaghue, had an entire class, and would enter them in competitions. All the girls—and there were twenty-five of them—would dance together, all wearing their special green costumes (green is one of the colors of Ireland—hence the Emerald Isle) with white lace collars, an orange pleat in the skirt (orange is the other color of Ireland), and plenty of embroidery on the front. In fact, it wasn't just Sinead from the O'Carroll family who studied with Ms. Donaghue; her younger sister Elaine also took classes, and the two of them danced together for a number of years.

Back then, Sinead's hair was much darker than it is now, quite brown in fact. Not that she's an artificial blonde now. The color has simply lightened over the years.

After several years of Irish dancing, Sinead was ready for new challenges, and once she became a teenager, she started classes in both jazz and tap dancing. It was something she loved, and her natural talent had grown. It became apparent that she might even be able to make a living as a dancer one day, which would have been one of her great dreams. She'd always seen herself as up there on the stage, a star of some kind.

"From the age of seven I imagined I'd be doing interviews one day. My mum used to say things to me like, 'Sinead, you're not on stage now,' but I'd be daydreaming and wouldn't really hear her!"

Everything about the stage enthralled Sinead. While other kids whiled away their summers doing nothing, Sinead would be attending Newbridge College, taking classes in music and drama, and having parts in their productions, including the Wizard in *The Wizard of Oz*. Then, to complement her dance classes, in her free time (!) she took classes in speech and drama from a woman named Edele Mulligan. Being up there under the lights was all she ever really wanted to do, and while her mother might have tried to bring her back down to earth, both her parents were actually very supportive of her dreams.

Those dreams of being on the stage came one small step closer when Sinead turned fifteen. That was when she began lessons in jazz dance and ballet. This wasn't in Newbridge, however, but in Dublin, which meant she had to commute into the city from home. While fifteen was late to begin ballet, what she really needed was the basics to be able to round out her dance education and add to her arsenal of graceful moves. Obviously, she wouldn't have gone this far without showing real talent and promise. While it seemed very adult to her, taking the bus into the center of Dublin for her classes, it was what she needed to progress in this. She was excited about the possibilities with dance. She loved it, she excelled, and she honestly believed that this was where her future lay. She was still making good grades at school, and enjoyed it, but the idea of college did nothing for her. Her heart was with dance, and the idea of being on the stage.

The big leap came when she was entered for a dance scholarship. This was really serious. It would mean no more school, but learning full-time about dance. And it would be in London, far away from home, but really the best place for her to learn with some of the top professionals around, what she'd really need if this was going to become her livelihood as well as her art.

She was on edge for weeks, waiting for the mailman every day to hear whether she'd won the scholarship. When the news that it was hers came through, she was overjoyed! Now, finally, she was really on the road to becoming a professional dancer. It was going to be difficult, leaving her parents, but in her heart she knew it would all be worthwhile.

The London Studio Centre was a prestigious dance school, one of the very best in England. A lot of people who'd studied there had gone on to perform in shows in the West End, on television, and to become choreographers.

The curriculum was tough, and they demanded a lot from their students. But in return, they taught virtually the whole spectrum of dance. In fact, Sinead said, about the only type of dancing they didn't teach there was breakdancing!

The Centre was in the King's Cross area of London, not the city's most salubrious area. But Sinead didn't care. Her parents found her a room with a nice family, and saw that she was settled in and comfortable. For herself, she didn't care what kind of neighborhood the Centre was in; simply to be going there, to be learning so much made life fulfilling. Every single day was a joy. She was sixteen, and full of all the possibilities of her life. More than that, she had all of London to go at. There was the nightlife, the shopping, all the sights to see.

As years go, that one was brilliant for her. Not only was she learning and pushing ahead, she was growing as a person. Away from home, she was learning a lot about how to cope alone, something she'd need for the future. She missed her family, of course, and talked to them on the phone and traveled home for the holidays, but it was as if she'd blossomed into an adult.

But the scholarship was for just a year. She'd made huge improvements in her technique, but the question was, was she ready to risk it all by staying in London and trying to make it as a dancer? She was just seventeen, and that, her parents thought, was still just a bit too young to be on her own, possibly starving in a big city a long way from home.

And Sinead agreed. London would still be there when she was ready to conquer it properly. It wasn't as if Dublin was without shows and opportunities for her. It even contained her favorite place in the world, Sandymount ("I love it there, it's so beautiful"). Better to start off in Dublin, become a big fish in a small pond, and then try her luck in the bigger pond.

So Sinead moved back home. Of course, after having had so much freedom, it wasn't quite the same, but she loved being around her family again; it was a warm, comfortable feeling, and she realized just how close to them all she was. After a few months, though, she realized how much she'd enjoyed being on her own, and compromised, taking a tiny apartment in Dublin.

The first thing she had to do was look for work. Not just as a dancer, but also something to bring in some money, a day job. Not that she had any career in mind beyond entertaining. Any day job she took on would be just something to help support her until she made a living from her art. And so there was a succession of small jobs. She tried her hand at telemarketing, was an attendant in a cinema, and even worked retail for a little while, in a store called Angel's. Meanwhile she was going to every audition she heard about, and got some parts at a couple of theaters in the city for shows, the Olympia and the Gate, as well as a few appearances as an extra on Irish television shows. It was a modest start, but a start nonetheless.

The jobs, she knew and believed with all her heart, would only be temporary. As she said, "I'm stubborn, ambitious, and earthy, you could say I'm a country girl at heart." And that country heart, and her drive, were going to make her succeed.

She continued to work at the theaters, even though the money wasn't much. But it made her feel as if she was achieving something. And she also took some classes at the Digges Lane Dance Centre, just to keep her technique strong. Also working out there were some other girls. Lindsay Aramou would occasionally drop by, and so would Keavy and Edele Lynch, who were part of a dance team, and constantly learning, and trying to improve as dancers. The four of them knew each other in a very casual way, just to say hello and things like that. They'd never stopped and chatted, and didn't even know if they had anything in common.

Sinead might have been a girl who was driven, but she wasn't someone who was capable of driving herself, it seemed. Naturally, her father had a van for his electrical business, and the family also had a car, which Barbara used a great deal. She'd tried to encourage Sinead to start driving, so she wouldn't be so reliant on public transport to get home from Dublin at night. Sinead did sign up for driving lessons (in Ireland and Britain, there's no such thing as drivers' education in schools), but quickly gave up, because being behind the wheel left her "too frightened"—it might be hard to believe, but it's true. So, after that brief experience, she was a girl who was driven, both metaphorically and literally!

When she had free time, if she wasn't hanging out in her apartment playing George Michael records and singing along (she'd been a fan since his days with Wham!, and he's still her favorite because he's "really cool and very talented"), she'd sometimes go and run errands with her mother. One day in 1996, Barbara had to drop her car off to have some work done on it. The place she always took it was a garage owned by a man named Brendan Lynch. While Barbara waited to talk to Brendan, Sinead was just passing the time, and happened to notice a vaguely familiar face emerging from the hood of a car. It was Keavy, whom she'd seen at Digges Lane. Keavy Lynch was Brendan's daughter, and after leaving school had started work for her dad, learning to become a mechanic. The two of them began chatting, mostly about what they both did at the Dance Centre, and they quickly learned that they both had the same dream—to perform.

As a dancer, of course, Sinead was highly trained, and making some money from it. Keavy and Edele had their dancing going on, and Keavy had another friend, Lindsay, whom she'd met in a kickboxing class, and who also sometimes went to Digges Lane. Somehow or other, someone suggested that the four of them meet and see what happened ... and B*Witched was born!

Of course, the band has become much bigger than any of them could ever have guessed the first time they got together at Digges Lane, and Sinead's dream of being onstage and giving interviews has become a daily reality. She's seen the world, talked to so many reporters and been on more television shows than she ever knew existed. It's a busy world she lives in these days.

The girls still share the same house in Surrey, outside London, that they moved into when they first came to England. It's been such a whirlwind of a time that there's been no chance to look for anywhere else. And they're so rarely there these days that it hardly matters, anyway. Home is pretty much just a place to sleep when they come off the road for a few days. And, given any spare time, Sinead, like the others, heads back to Ireland to see her family and friends. When she's home, though, there's absolutely no star treatment for her from her parents or siblings.

"As soon as I get home, Mum sends me out for her shopping!" Sinead said. And although she gets recognized on the street in Newbridge—she's the local girl who's made it big—she never feels different there.

"I'm not sure anyone ever really feels famous," she pointed out. "You don't feel any different inside—you're just the same person. You don't wake up one morning and think, 'Ah-ha, now I'm famous!'"

Of course, to their fans, B*Witched *are* famous. But they've been very lucky.

"We haven't had any bad fan experiences," Sinead said. "Generally, they're quite nice. There's a group in England that always meets us at the airport and gives us travel sweets when we go on long journeys. We've gotten weird presents, though. I got a half-pound of butter."

And presents don't come much stranger than that! It turned out that there was a reason behind it.

"I think I said on the TV once that I liked Irish butter," Sinead explained, "so this girl turned up outside the station with a half-pound of Irish butter. I used it."

Well, what else could she do?

And, of course, to Edele, Keavy, and Lindsay, she certainly isn't famous. She's just one of the girls, the same as the rest of them. While they usually get along very well, they all have their little foibles that annoy the others. If there's ever a fight in the B*Witched house, it's usually over... salt. Yes, salt (so you can tell it's nothing major). Evidently Edele loves her salt, and puts it on everything, which means she and Sinead can never cook together—Sinead doesn't use the stuff.

Unlike boy bands, most of whom seem to live off fast food and junk food, these girls know how to take care of themselves. Sinead is actually quite adept in the kitchen, thanks to her mother's teaching and home economics at school. She loves Italian food, and her specialty dish is tagliatelle carbonara—noodles and sauce, all from scratch. The only problem, though, is that "the other girls don't like it." Not that a little thing like that stops her making it. Instead she just gets to eat it all herself! But one thing she won't put into the dish is olives—she can't stand them.

Mind you, Sinead isn't one for a big, cooked breakfast. When she gets up, the thing that gets her going is a bowl of Sugar Puffs drowned in some very cold milk, along with a slice of toast. When she's on the road, and she can't get her favorite cereal, she makes do with a banana to set her up for the day. And even Sugar Puffs have gone off the menu lately, since she stopped eating sugar (and that means no dougnuts, either).

Of course, traveling so much means that the girls do sometimes eat fast food (they have a cook who travels with them and often makes home-cooked meals, but that's not always possible). Sinead likes stopping at McDonald's, where her order is "normally a Big Mac, but lately it's been chicken nuggets with barbecue sauce."

Her big fault, she admits, is "I annoy the others when I stand in front of the TV at home." That usually happens when she's watching sports—she loves gymnastics and horse racing—the British soaps, like *Coronation Street* and her favorite, *Eastenders*—"I love it when we have an evening off and get to see it!" That doesn't happen too much any more, and like any soap, you need to keep track of what's going on.

The house the girls rent is actually quite small, with just two bedrooms and one bathroom, which means plenty of sharing. Sinead and Edele share one of the bedrooms, the sunny bedroom at the front, where Edele's bed is by the window, and Sinead's over by the wardrobe (this being England, the houses tend to have wardrobes rather than built-in closets). At least the wine-colored carpet tends to hide any stains!

If there's one great luxury Sinead enjoys about being in the house, it's the chance to take a long, relaxing bath.

"We're always in such a rush we only have time for showers," she explained. "It's fab when I get a chance to have a nice hot bath!" She puts lavender oil in the water for a complete pampering experience.

Obviously, the girls don't get much time off. But sometimes they'll manage to squeeze a day here and there. Right before Christmas last year, a friend of Sinead's, R.K., came over to London from Ireland, and the two of them took the train up to London for a serious day of shopping in Oxford Street and the trendiest little stores they could find—including such fancy places as Prada and Harvey Nichols in Knightsbridge. It was a real shop-till-you-drop affair, and Sinead loved every second of it, although she was exhausted by the time they got back to Surrey, laden down with parcels.

You might have noticed that all of the girls in B*Witched wear specially made rings of silver, each with a charm dangling by a chain. The charm is their symbol, and those symbols crop up everywhere. Sinead's is a shamrock, for Ireland, a constant reminder of home, which is still very important to her, even if she doesn't have much time to see it these days.

"I know it might sound a little bit sad, but I really do like living in Ireland," she said. "It's my dream to have a big house by the sea there someday." That's a dream with a very good chance of coming true.

And if you've looked carefully at pictures of Sinead, you might have noticed a curious thing. Some show her with a tattoo around her neck, while others show her without. Before and after shots, perhaps? Not at all. While Sinead likes the look of a tattoo, the idea of the pain involved in getting one doesn't appeal to her at all (you'll note that she doesn't have any piercings, either). So she actually collects and uses fake tattoos, and the one around her neck has been a prime—and very convincing—example of that. It's like having the best of both worlds.

While the girls have played up their tomboy reputation a lot, that doesn't mean they completely ignore the girlie things. Sometimes the four of them will have a quiet night in, giving each other facials, eating chocolate, with the television on in the background. But once in a while a girl will need something like that.

While she's not a slave to cosmetics or anything like that, Sinead has to pay attention to her appearance—it's what's expected of her. And she does love her lipstick. In fact, according to Keavy, in the B*Witched house, Sinead is the one who spends the most time in front of the mirror: "Not because she's vain, but because she loves lipstick. She won't go out without her lipstick on." And she has a favorite shampoo, KNF, which comes from the trendy McMillan's salon in the Covent Garden area of London. And, like any girl, she has her fave clothes, too. In her case, "I have a nice black chiffon dress which I bought from Morgan. It's got a little hole cut away at the back."

One thing Sinead pays real attention to is her nails, even if they are false. In fact, apart from lip balm, it's one thing she's always sure to carry in her purse. "I never leave home without spares," she said firmly. "You never know when one is going to come unstuck and fall off!" That actually happened to her once. Unfortunately, it was during an interview, and it came off while she was playing with her hair, and the false nail ended up stuck in her hair—she didn't even know! Talk about embarrassing!

Then again, it's impossible to go through life without a few embarrassing moments, and Sinead has had her share. Probably the worst occurred during a B*Witched show.

"There was water on the stage and I slipped and landed on my behind." That would have been bad enough, but a television presenter was there, and later mentioned it to the whole country on her show, just to add to the indignity.

Among the other girls in B*Witched, Sinead is infamous for being forgetful.

"Sinead takes everyone's stuff and puts it in her bag," pointed out Edele. "When you ask for it back, she goes, 'I don't have it!'"

"She goes, 'I swear I put it back,'" continued Keavy. "Ten minutes later she's like, 'Oh, I do have it.'"

And Lindsay added, "She's forever leaving things behind at hotels. In the space of one week she lost two jackets, a pair of jeans and a B*Witched ring!"

By now the others make allowances for Sinead's memory, and even play tricks on her about it. One time they were all getting ready to leave for the airport to catch a plane. Sinead supposedly had all the tickets in her purse, and when the others asked, she assured them that they were in her possession. What she didn't know what that the girls had taken them back—just to be sure. When they got to check-in, Sinead was frantically searching for the tickets. After a couple of minutes, though, the others clued her in as to what they'd done—and gave Sinead her own ticket back!

Finding time for guys is something of a problem for Sinead these days—she simply doesn't have any! How could it be otherwise right now? She might drool over Matthew Perry, Christian Slater, and, above all, Matthew McConaughey ("He's pure class," she announced once), but in real life she's dateless. Not by choice, but because of schedule. And for now that's fine; she's in no hurry to settle down.

"I'm waiting 'til I'm thirty," she said. "God knows who it'll be, though—the next person who drops out of the sky! I'd love to have children, but then I think of the pain! I can't even go to the dentist!"

While it's still a long way off, the idea of marriage is something she takes very seriously.

"I think if you really want to get married, you have to work at making it happen," she noted. But that won't be for a long time yet. She might miss having a fella, but there's her career to focus on for right now.

When the chance for a vacation does come, you'll either find Sinead heading back to Ireland, or popping off to another part of Europe. On her travels with the band, she fell in love with Italy (well, she already loved the food!), and wants to explore more of it as the chances arise. Why Italy? Well, "because of the food, fashion, and architecture—it's completely different from the rest of Europe."

When you get down to it, Sinead understands what makes B*Witched so popular. Apart from the music, she said, "We're the same as our fans, it's the secret of our success! We're young and we love having fun and wearing nice clothes. Also, we believe in ourselves, which is really important."

And that faith in her own abilities is what kept Sinead going for so long and taking classes in dance. It's something she would advise for everyone who's interested in a career in music—or in anything, for that matter.

"The main thing to do is just believe in yourself, and keep working at your dream. And keep working hard." With talent, perseverance, and ambition (plus a little Irish luck), almost anything is possible.

Without the fans, however, it would never have happened, and all the girls realize that. They think their fans are the best in the world, and truly appreciate them. Right now, as Sinead said, "We're having the time of our lives, and we [want] to thank every one of you so much.''

Not only modest, but also polite...what more could you ask for from a pop star? But if there's one thing for certain, it's that Sinead—and the other girls in B*Witched—will be making music and dancing for a long time to come. They've barely scratched the surface of what they want to do. And who knows—maybe we'll see Sinead doing that solo dance onstage yet!

Edele

"I ALWAYS WISH ON THE first star I see," said Edele. "Sometimes I wish for my family to be happy or that I can go home and see them. I also wish that B*Witched will do well and stay together."

Of the three wishes Edele likes to make, there's only one that's a problem these days—getting home to see her family. With three of their kids as major pop stars, Brendan and Noeleen Lynch have every reason to be happy. And B*Witched have done very well so far, and that shows absolutely no sign of changing in the foreseeable future.

As every B*Witched fan knows, Edele and Keavy Lynch are twins—Keavy is actually the older by a few seconds, but the girls are identical. When they were born, on December 15, 1979, in Dublin, their parents already had three children, two girls—Tara and Allison—and a boy, Shane. And that would not be the sum total, either. In another couple of years there was yet another sister, Naomi, making for a real house-full for the Lynch family.

Edele Claire Christina Edwina Lynch, to give Edele her full name (and try saying that quickly three times!), was a very active little girl. As soon as she could walk, she'd be out in the garden running around. Once she learned to swim, that kept her occupied, and as soon as she was old enough, she took up gymnastics, which rapidly became her major fixation. "I always thought I might like to be an

Olympic gymnast," she said, and it was a real ambition of hers. In fact, she became very good at the sport through talent and constant practicing, and even performed on Irish national television when she was young.

The twins were very close when they were young, and are still that way today. As babies and toddlers, their mother dressed them in matching clothes, making it almost impossible to tell them apart. In fact, the only real thing that distinguishes Edele from Keavy is the scar Edele has across the bridge of her nose. When she was little it was quite obvious, but it's faded as she's grown up.

It all happened at the twins' third birthday party—not the best present anyone's ever received! Edele and Keavy, being young and full of energy, were running around, acting totally mad, and pretending to be airplanes flying in the living room. The problem came when Edele accidentally crashed, slipping and banging her head against the concrete of the fireplace.

Naturally, she was taken off to the hospital, crying and bleeding all over the place, and in need of stitches (a total of eighteen by the time the doctor had finished with her). Aunt Ann stayed home to watch Keavy, who spent the whole time crying in sympathy with her sister, and saying that her head hurt, too—a kind of bond quite common in identical twins.

Although the teachers wanted to separate the girls when they started school, the Lynches insisted on them being together in the same class, which immediately made Edele feel more at ease, and helped her become the chatterbox she still is today. She was a good student, generally getting above average grades, but opting for subjects that definitely weren't girlie, like metal shop—in fact, she was the only girl in her school to take metal work, which left her feeling somewhat embarrassed. It paid off in the end, though. Even now, she can still make metal jewelry, and has been known to transform a table fork into an arm bracelet. She also proved to be quite good at art. Apart from that, she seemed happiest riding her skateboard. "I used to ride it outside our house for hours," she recalled.

Music was always a part of life in the family. Wherever you turned, it was there. Edele's first record was "Billie Jean" by Michael Jackson, a single from his massive-selling *Thriller* album, that she saved up and bought when she was five years old. But it wasn't just pop music that was in the air around the Lynch house. Being Ireland, there were all types of music being made. Noeleen played guitar and sang, and two of the girls' uncles were drummers.

"Our grandad played the fiddle," Edele recalled, "so we never needed much of an excuse to dance and sing. From a really early age, we started making up our own songs and performing them. I suppose, at some point, it occurred to us that we might grow up to be performers. But it seemed like a distant dream."

Of course, back then they weren't taking it seriously, either. They had plenty of things on their minds, like just being kids, although their mum and dad were always supportive of anything their kids wanted to do.

"They always told us to follow our dreams and have had a huge influence of my life. They're very important to me."

That kind of support might well explain why Edele and Keavy are in B*Witched now, Shane is in Boyzone, while Naomi has gone on to become a European dancing champion, Tara is making her way as a member of a band called Fab!, and Allison has moved to Boston and become a computer engineer.

The twins were generally very well behaved in school, but there were inevitably times when they couldn't resist pulling a few jokes. The most memorable occurred with a teacher called Miss Hickey. She'd been with the girls for three years, and insisted she could tell them apart. That proved to be wishful thinking. When the girls switched places, she soon discovered that they seemed completely identical, after all.

Like so many girls, Edele started taking ballet classes, which she thoroughly enjoyed, and proved to be quite good at. However, she had absolutely no ambitions to become a ballerina, and soon joined her older sister, Tara, in jazz dance classes. The idea of entertaining people was something she genuinely loved, whether it was dancing, gymnastics, or whatever. Whenever auditions were held for a new school play, Edele would be there, trying to win a part. She simply loved being on the stage, although becoming a pop star was something that hadn't really come into her mind, and wouldn't for a few years yet, even though she loved singing, and could somehow imagine herself doing that.

Dancing really seemed to be her main interest, along with gymnastics. And she might have fulfilled that dream of becoming an Olympic gymnast—she really was that good—until she was forced to quit by an injury. "I hurt my knee when I was thirteen and had to give it up," she explained. That didn't mean she had to stop dancing, though. Quite the contrary—she spent more and more time on it, and formed a disco-dancing team, which they named Starlight, along with Keavy, Tara, and their friend Pamela.

Unlikely as it might sound, it was popular in Ireland, and the girls did very well. Noeleen made their costumes, which always looked very cool. With black and white fringes flying as they moved, they all looked very impressive indeed. That was only one of their dance activities, though. Along with some other friends, the twins put together a hip-hop dance group that went under the name of BOOM and made money playing various promotional events, including gigs for big brand names like Sony PlayStation and Coca-Cola. If that wasn't quite enough, both of them were soon teaching classes at Digges Lane Dance Centre, the place where they'd received their training.

Starlight entered a lot of dance competitions, but never won anything. Still, it seemed to be leading to bigger and better things, so Edele wasn't complaining. But it wasn't making her into a star.

However, she was seeing stardom in the family, thanks to her brother, Shane. His band, Boyzone, had gone on to great things indeed, topping the charts in Ireland and Britain with their ballads (to date, they've had a total of five Number One hits, all ballads, because, they claim, they "can't dance"). Edele got a great education, secondhand, watching all the things her brother was going through, and hearing his stories. One thing it definitely didn't do was put her off music. In school she'd taken up the flute, although she was never *that* great on the instrument, but she could get by in the band.

The Lynches always took big family vacations, even when the kids were small. While their favorite destination was Portugal, where the kids could all romp on the long, open beaches, when the twins were young, the whole family went to America. Since then, of course, Edele and Keavy have been back several times (and now they're old enough to remember it!), but vacations were always something to look forward to. Whenever school was out, the family would try to take off somewhere. They had a boat, which proved to be very useful in touring the lovely rivers of Ireland.

While Edele continued to make good grades, it was apparent that she had absolutely no interest in continuing at school and going on to university. She was bright, but not especially academic, and English, in particular, bored her. "I hate reading," she said. "I never read." So, when she was sixteen, after finishing the school year, it was agreed that she would quit school (in Ireland and the U.K., leaving school at sixteen is fairly common for pupils who don't plan on attending university).

The question was, what would she do with her life? She had her dancing, and her dreams of making it. And since seeing what Shane was doing, the idea of becoming a singer had grown bigger and bigger in her mind. She was musical, and she could sing—why not? If she ever managed to get a band together, then the sky would be the limit, she thought. And Shane was more than willing to offer advice to his sisters.

"He wanted to make sure we knew it was hard work, but he never stopped us. He let us learn on our own because it's the best way."

That was all well and good, but it didn't pay the bills. For now she needed to start looking for work. It wasn't long before she found something—working retail in a sporting goods store named Stadium Sports. It wasn't glamorous, it wasn't high paying, but it was honest work with a wage packet, and that was all that mattered—for now.

It wasn't a wild, party life she led, though. Between work and dancing, her time was pretty much filled; there weren't even many boys in her life, perhaps, as she'd recall later, because "I can't flirt. I wouldn't want to send out those kind of signals anyway. I've only had someone ask me to dinner once and that was years ago when I was working in a sports shop." So Stadium Sports was good for one thing, apart from money!

It was grand being a part of Starlight. It kept her active and fit, and they did perform regularly. Between that, BOOM, and teaching dance classes, Edele led a very active life. But it wasn't as fulfilling as she wanted. Her biggest buzz came from being up on stage and entertaining people. She'd continued playing the flute, and had joined a marching band called the Dublin Allstars. With them, she visited New York to play in the St. Patrick's Day Parade—her second trip to the U.S., and another major event in her life. Still, it wasn't quite enough. Now, more and more, she wanted to sing to people. And she simply didn't have an outlet for that. Something that combined her dancing with singing would be perfect, she reckoned; all she had to do was find it.

So when fate came knocking, in the form of Sinead and

Keavy, Edele was more than up for it. And once Lindsay became a part of the package, it was obvious that everything was going to work perfectly. Maybe they could get to be as big as Shane and Boyzone, Edele thought at night, after the girls had spent an evening rehearsing and writing songs. That would have seemed like mega success; little did she imagine just how much bigger they'd become, and how quickly.

Before the girls did their first showcase, Brendan and Noeleen gave Edele a teddy bear for luck. She named him Patch, and even now he goes everywhere with her, her personal lucky charm. He really seems to have worked, too, as the girls have gone on to be huge—a far cry from those evenings in Digges Lane when they tried to work out routines to the sound of a boom box.

It's a long way from being a shop assistant at Stadium Sports to jetting first-class all over the world, and sometimes it seems as if it's all just happened in a heartbeat. Edele has barely had a chance to catch her breath since it all started. Everything has just moved faster and faster, until it's become something of a blur. Along the way, apart from hit singles, albums going platinum all over the world, and a packed concert schedule, there's also been a lot of fun. Well, who wouldn't enjoy having their dream come true? And, in the process, entertaining millions of people. Edele gets to sing—she's the band's lead singer, just in case you didn't already know—and dance; the best of both worlds, as far as she's concerned. And she loves it. "I never, ever, *ever* want to go back to the sports shop again!"

Life might have the occasional down moment, like not seeing her family too often—she actually sees a lot of Shane on the road—but there are plenty of compensations, like the chance to often eat her favorite meal of seafood.

"Lobster, crayfish, prawns, winkles? I love them all," Edele laughed. "If I see or smell lobster, I just have to have some. You could say I'm lobster mad." And her love of seafood isn't just limited to restaurant meals. When she orders out, Edele usually goes for Chinese—and every time it's king prawns with mushrooms.

Not that being in the band, with all they've achieved so quickly, has fulfilled quite *all* Edele's ambitions. She's seen the world, had hits—but she's never jumped out of an airplane. Yes, that's right, Edele would like to try skydiving one day. Which certainly sounds odd, given that she won't even go on a rollercoaster (even stranger, when you consider that their second U.K. Number One single was called "Rollercoaster"). And maybe she'll do it—but hopefully not in the near future.

When B*Witched moved to England, it was a huge transition for Edele. Neither she nor Keavy had lived away from home before. Being close to all the members of their family, they both tended to spend a lot of time on the phone with friends and relations. And, since living away from her folks, Edele decided to get a family for Patch, to the point, Sinead said, where "You can't see her bed for teddies," which Edele admits is true. "I've collected most of them since I moved over here to England. I can't resist a teddy bear—if I see a teddy machine, I have to win one!"

Like her sister and Sinead, Edele likes to watch the British soap operas (which all air in the evening, not during the day), and sometimes she just spends an evening lounging around in front of the television. If you should happen to turn up at their house on a day they're not working, you won't find Edele looking as glam as she normally does.

"When we get a day off, we never wear any makeup," she admitted. "People think it's great to get your hair and makeup done all the time, but after two years of an hour and a half every day, it gets a bit annoying." It's just that tomboy side of them all getting a chance to shine through.

If you ever wondered how it is that Edele and Keavy are identical twins, but have different hair colors, well, there's a simple answer. They were both born brunettes, but when the band really got going, Edele, as the front woman, changed her shade.

"I'd wanted to have red hair for a long time, so I just got it," she admitted. And why not. After all, you can have your hair any color you like these days—although don't expect to see a blonde Edele anytime soon (she did, however, once don a blue wig for a special performance)!

Like anyone else, Edele has her favorite clothes. In her case it's "my Motor jeans—they're square, patchy ones, and I love them." But of all the girls, she's the one who's most into denim. There's very rarely a time you'll see her not wearing at least one piece of denim on her body, and usually more, along with her trainers. It's a casual, funky look, but she's a casual kind of girl, even if the others say she's the most fashion-conscious of the lot! Or maybe she's only fashion-conscious when it comes to clothes made out of denim!

While she's still something of a chatterbox, there are times when Edele can bring down the house, quite literally. It happened in Surrey once, at the house they all share.

"I was getting ready to go to a party," she recalled, "and I was trying to fix my hair while standing on the upstairs landing. It wouldn't go right, so I started to jump up and down in frustration. Then I heard a crash and the light had fallen out of the ceiling downstairs!"

Luckily, nowadays she only brings down the house in concert. But once in a while disaster can strike there, too, like the occasion during a show when her jeans split.

"I had to dance with my back to the audience for the rest of the song," she laughed. But she was at least enough of a trouper to carry on for the song before she went and quickly changed.

While the Irish have a reputation as drinkers, you certainly wouldn't know it from Edele. Guinness may be the national beverage, but it never crosses her lips. But there is some liquid she loves to consume, and that's milk. It's not unusual for her to go through a quart, or even three pints, in a single day. She just loves the stuff, and it certainly doesn't seem to have had any adverse effect on her! And since she loves milk, ice cream figures high up on her list of favorite foods, particularly vanilla: "It has to be yellow, though, because it tastes better." And, coincidentally enough, cheery yellow just happens to be her favorite color.

All the girls have their special B*Witched rings, and Edele's is a B, for B*Witched. It's not as if she's the leader of the band—there isn't such a person, really—it's just the symbol that seems to really reflect her. Like Patch, the ring goes everywhere with her. But unlike Sinead, she's never lost hers!

Now that she's famous, she's discovered what Shane already knew—that it makes absolutely no difference to who you really are.

"I thought fame might change me as a person, but it hasn't—not even slightly. It made us excited for a while and we were proud that we'd achieved what we set out to do, but it didn't really change us as people."

Edele has really taken on the role of house mother in Surrey, even though she's not the oldest. But she's the one who seems to work best with people, and be the best negotiator.

"Edele is a very strong person," Keavy pointed out. "We all go to Edele 'cause she knows how to talk to people and how to handle everybody. She knows how to say things."

And she's not backward about speaking her mind, either. If something bothers her, she doesn't keep it inside. One perfect example happened on a flight B*Witched were taking.

"The steward asked if I wanted a bread roll, and by mistake I touched one without taking it. When he came back he was really rude, so I had to tell him off. He was really sorry at the end of it."

When it comes to fellas, too, Edele knows what she likes, and doesn't like. And her tastes can be a little bit odd. "They look better when they're scruffy or dirty," she said. "As long as their socks are clean, I'm not bothered!" That doesn't mean she's not picky, however. Her two pin-ups are Jason Priestley, "because he's cute," and more recently "I've got the hots for David Charvet, who used to be in *Baywatch*. He's very cute and sporty as well! Mmmm . . ."

Not that she's in any hurry to settle down. Life is simply too busy right now to even think of a boyfriend. And while all the boy bands might get hordes of screaming girls after them, the reverse isn't true. You won't find too many boys yelling for B*Witched or the Spices. If they fancy them, they tend to keep it quiet. And Edele, like the rest of the girls, is naturally wary of any male fan asking for a date, because they might only want to know them because they're big stars. Mostly, however, the problem is just time. There's just not the luxury of being able to get to know someone properly.

"You don't have any time to spend with him except over the phone. And it can be quite difficult over the phone, especially when you first get to know someone."

Apart from being wary of male fans, the only thing that really scares Edele is spiders; she totally hates them. "I'd only ever hit one of the other girls if they had a spider in their hair," she said. Arachnophobia aside, Edele loves animals, and ducks in particular. She and Keavy actually have two ducks (one of which supposedly hates water, believe it or not!) that still live at their parents' house.

Of course, no one, not even Edele, is perfect. Close maybe, but she does have one bad habit—she likes to tap her foot all the time when she's doing something, and it just drives the rest of the girls absolutely crazy.

"It's really annoying!" said Lindsay. "We're always telling her to stop!" Does it work? Well, let's just say she doesn't do it as often as she used to, but the habit is still there. And, of course, she does have some phrases that she overuses. The main ones are "That drives me mad!" and "Have a hoolie!" (*hoolie* is Irish slang for party). For herself, Edele sees her biggest fault as being that "I'm stubborn and it drives everyone mad!"

But being stubborn and willing to work has helped the girls get where they are today, so it's obviously paid off in a very big way.

While most guys wouldn't find many problems with Edele's looks, she does—at least with her shoe size. It seems she thinks her feet are too big. "I'd like them to be size three but they're five-and-a-half. I want them to be dainty and cute!" Not that they're large now, but a three would be minute!

Even though she gets to hear all types of music, and meets all types of bands, Edele remains a major Backstreet Boys fan (although they'll never replace Boyzone as her favorite boy band, for obvious reasons). She also likes the Spice Girls, which some people would find odd, given the tag B*Witched have been given as "the Irish Spice Girls." It's not true, of course, but it doesn't worry Edele one bit. They know the differences. The two bands have actually met, and got along fine—and why shouldn't they? There's room for more than one girl-pop band on the charts, especially when they both do such good work. And while there were rumors that B*Witched simply started to copy the Spices, those have finally been put to rest. B*Witched started *before* the Spice Girls first hit with "Wannabe."

"We admire the Spice Girls for what they've done," Edele explained, "and they've opened up such a big door for girl bands. But it wasn't any band in particular that influenced us because ever since we started with each other, we just wanted something different. We knew something different had to be done, something that hadn't really been done before, and I think Irish music is quite different. Every song we do has something different to offer which is what we want to do. We don't want to be under one category of music."

Which may be why Edele is such a fan of the Corrs, the Irish band made up of three sisters and a brother. Like B*Witched, they put a little bit of the Irish into everything they do, but they're not an "Irish" band. Instead, they tackle all kinds of music. And, like B*Witched, they've become one of the Emerald Isle's biggest exports in the last couple of years, selling a ton of records around the world. Unlike B*Witched, though, they've yet to crack America!

A lot of girls, though, would feel the pressure of being a role model to so many younger girls to be a very terrifying responsibility. For Edele, however, "it doesn't feel that way at all, because we have quite a positive image. The way we are naturally is okay for kids to watch. We've had a lot of mothers come up to us and say, 'You're great role models for my children.'" And that has to be a very satisfying feeling.

Take a stealthy look through Edele's purse, and you'll find that she always carries her multivitamins—when you're on the go that much you need vitamins—and a pendant, a cross on a broken chain that Keavy gave her years before and that she takes everywhere with her. She'd never get rid of it (or a lot of other things) because she is "completely, totally, and utterly" superstitious. Given that the address of the girls' house is 13, you have to wonder how she feels about that, though... although it would seem that thirteen has ended up being a lucky number for them!

Sinead might be off sugar, but not Edele. She's sweet, but she likes things sweeter—two sugars please in her tea and coffee. You might remember that if you run into her in a restaurant sometime. And if she happens to be eating a sandwich, the chances are it will be chicken "with loads of mayonnaise. It has to be on white bread, though!"

While Edele isn't one for usually dwelling on the more serious side of life (her favorite movie is *Clueless*, "because it's so funny"), that doesn't mean she's an airhead. When it comes to the band she can get very serious indeed.

"I'm levelheaded, friendly, and ambitious," she announced. "I'm also a bit of a perfectionist and can be secretive." Well, maybe not that secretive, but a perfectionist she definitely is. And, to get anywhere in music, you have to be ambitious. Now that she's a star, making a lot of money, she contributes part of her income to a couple of hospices back in Ireland, although she doesn't really publicize her charitable work. There's no need; it's a very private thing.

Eddie, as the others call her, is as friendly as she claims. Meet her and she'll sweep you off your feet with her personality. That's what makes her the ideal frontwoman for the band. The girl has got charisma to spare. On the stage, she's the obvious focal point, even in the more complicated dance routines. And her strong voice is the ideal vehicle for the lyrics—most of which the girls write themselves.

There's no side to her, as they say in Ireland. She doesn't put on airs and graces, just because she's up there, and the audience is down below. What you see is really what you get with Edele. If it's a big occasion, she might put glittery stars on her face, but that's about as dressed up as she's likely to get. She's down to earth, and she was born with a great deal of common sense.

Things have gone well for her, for all the girls. But in large part, her success has been due to hard work and determination—not to mention oodles of talent. She'll admit that their success is "really great, but it's not any trick, it just went out this way. People like our songs, and they get happy when they hear us. And then we get happy."

Which means that Edele has a lot to be happy about these days. Things have gone brilliantly so far, and they show no signs of fading. With a new album completed, a major American tour, and then their own headlining British tour this fall, Edele has plenty to keep herself busy. And you can bet that if she has her way, things won't ever be static. B*Witched will always be pushing at one boundary or another, trying to be the very best they can be—at everything they do. For Edele, there's simply no other way.

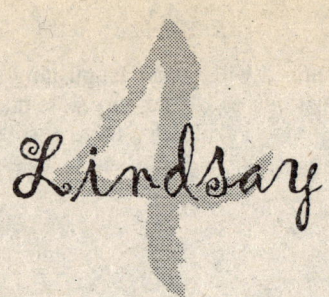

Lindsay

LINDS MIGHT WELL BE THE odd one out in the band, if any one of these female four musketeers can be considered an odd one out. She's the youngest by just over a year, having been born on December 18, 1980. And she's the only member of the band not to have been born and raised in Ireland (although you wouldn't know it from her accent); she was, in fact, born in Athens, Greece, and lived there until she was a teenager.

Lindsay Gael Christina Armaou might have a Greek name and upbringing, but she's always been half-Irish—her mum, Sharon, comes from Kildare. Sharon married Iannis Armaou, a man who owned a hotel in Athens, and settled there with him. Lindsay was the only child the couple would have. That could have easily made her into something of a spoiled brat, but her parents weren't about to let that happen.

With a Greek father and an Irish mother, Lindsay grew up bilingual, learning both Greek and English. The Greek would prove useful in years to come, when she took it for her Irish school leaving certificate. All those years of speaking it every day meant she coasted to a top grade.

To a lot of people, Athens is a city of ruins and history. While there is a lot of history in the buildings and even in the air, and the classical buildings like the Acropolis certainly catch the eye, Athens is every bit the twentieth-century metropolis, bustling with people and traffic, as big and cosmopolitan as any capital city anywhere, with more than its share of skyscrapers, suits, and cell phones.

Since her father ran a hotel, little Lindsay saw a lot of people passing through her home. In a way, it made up for not having any brothers or sisters to play with. And at school there were plenty of other kids—and plenty of birthday parties to attend.

Her performing began early, when she was in kindergarten, playing a fairy, in a short white dress and white wings. In those days, though, Lindsay had curly light brown hair. She was actually born with jet-black hair, which lightened as she grew, then turned darker again, until she was twelve, when it was dark and *very* straight. The curl didn't return until she moved to the damper climate of Ireland as a teenager. These days her natural hair color is a medium brown, but she actually dyes it a deeper shade—although she's not promising it'll always stay that way! Her eyes too, change color—"they go from green to orange to brown," she said, depending on her mood.

Even when she was small, music was very important to Lindsay. Back then, she loved it all, even the classical music her father would play. Lindsay's own tastes ran to pop, and she'd buy the releases by Madonna, Kylie Minogue, New Kids on the Block, and Michael Jackson—in fact, the first record she ever bought was Jackson's "Bad." When she was seven, Lindsay began piano lessons, and within a year she was performing at the school Christmas concert. In many ways, music was in her genes: Iannis played piano, and Sharon sang very well (her mother was also a very good dancer, another talent Lindsay seems to have inherited).

Even then, Linds had dreams of being a pop star. That's common in kids, but for her it was something different and more intense. She really felt it was a part of her future. She kept quiet about that, however, since it was expected that she'd do well academically—and she did. While math wasn't her best subject, she excelled in all the others, so much so that Sharon thought her daughter would benefit from a strong education in Ireland, and the chance of a place at a top university there.

Cats and Lindsay have always gone together. The family kept them when she was young, and when she was ten, she saved a litter of kittens from drowning in a Greek river. Even now her mother keeps two cats, Leah and Snoopy (as well as three dogs—Husky, Cheeky, and Chubby) for her daughter. So it's no surprise that Lindsay's symbol in the band is a black cat (black cat, witches, B*Witched—get it?), and there's a charm of a cat on her B*Witched ring.

The idea of leaving Greece and moving to Ireland with her mum and the cats was hard for Lindsay. While she'd been there before, to visit family, and she spoke English fluently, all she'd ever really known was Athens. Her friends were there, and everything familiar. She wasn't sure she wanted to leave, but Sharon knew that in the long run it would be for the best. The transition wouldn't be that bad, since Lindsay had been attending an English school in Athens.

Still, it was something of a culture shock, and it did take her a little while to adjust. Though Sharon was from Kildare, it somehow seemed natural to settle in Dublin, which, in its own way, was reminiscent of Athens, a real city with culture and opportunity and history. Since Iannis owned the hotel, there was no way he could move from Athens, which meant that Sharon and Lindsay were without him, although they called every day, and went to Greece for all the school holidays. And it was in Ireland that she saw snow for the very first time, which was quite a revelation for her. Making her first snowball and snowman, lying down and making her first snow angel, made her feel like a little girl again.

"It did get cold in Greece," she said, "but it very rarely rained and never snowed."

It was music that first helped Lindsay in Ireland. By then she'd been playing the piano for six years, and now she also took up the guitar, joining the school orchestra, and then the choir. She just thoroughly enjoyed performing for people, and thought it was the coolest thing going. So it was no surprise when she signed on for the musicals the school put on, finding herself with roles in productions like *Joseph and the Technicolor Dreamcoat* and dancing in *Little Shop of Horrors*. She would even go on to conduct the school orchestra.

While Sharon encouraged her daughter's musical interests, she was more interested in Lindsay getting the best education she could—that was why they'd moved, after all. The girl was exceedingly bright, and very well behaved. About the worst thing she ever did as a teenager was tell her mum she was staying at a friend's house when, in fact, she was going out to a party. And at school she rarely misbehaved—the only time she did anything bad was when she threw half a Mars bar across the room to a friend. She was caught by the teacher and sent outside for the rest of the period. You couldn't exactly call her a wild girl, then. She liked spending time with the friends she'd made, but time wasn't something she had too much of. Between her studies, the extracurricular activities, and going to Greece every vacation, there was hardly a spare moment in her life! No wonder, then, that she decided early that she didn't like to sleep.

"It just seems like such a waste of time," she said. "I hate sleeping, full stop!"

In her last year of school, Lindsay added something else to her list of activities—she began to study kick boxing. She no longer has the chance to pursue it, but she quickly rose to become a blue belt. And it was there she became friends with another student, Keavy Lynch, who also dreamed of becoming a pop star. There was quite a lot they had in common, really—including the fact that they'd both been huge New Kids on the Block fans.

Lindsay told her new friend about her dreams of being a pop star, and learned that Keavy wanted exactly the same thing. For Lindsay, though, it really looked as if her life would take another course. She'd gotten her Junior Certificate, and now she was in the process of working for her Leaving Certificate. If she did well in that, it would mean a place at college, and the chance to fulfill her mother's dreams. Lindsay already knew what she wanted to study—business. At the same time, she knew she wasn't about to abandon her real dream. She had a good voice, she understood music, and because of the kick boxing she moved well. Even if she ended up in college, she was determined she'd record some tracks and see what she could do with them.

When Linds tried for her Leaving Certificate, out of a possible six hundred points, she scored four hundred and sixty, far more than most students. It was enough to get her a place at Trinity College, the most prestigious university in Ireland. It looked as if she was set.

By then, though, the girls had been working on their band, and things were really starting to move. She had to make a choice between career and education.

"I always wanted to be a pop star," she admitted. "I had a place in college to go and study business, but when we got the recording contract I said, 'No, I'm going for it!'"

Well, if you didn't pursue your dreams when you were young, you'd spend the rest of your life wondering what if . . . ? In the end, Lindsay didn't turn down the college place she'd been offered, but, on her mother's advice, asked for a deferment for a year. That way she could see how things developed, and no doors were closed. But as the band really took off, she contacted Trinity and refused the place. Not that she wouldn't like to attend college one day. But if she does, it would be because she wanted to, to study something that really interested her, rather than as a career move.

When the girls first got together, Lindsay was still in high school, but left not long after. Since she wasn't going to college, and the band wasn't making any money yet, that meant she needed a job. Like Edele, she took the retail option, working at a store called Julien's in St. Stephen's shopping center in Dublin. It was the scene of one of her worst moments, one she still can't think about without cringing. She'd worn jeans to work, bent over, and the seam parted on the seat.

"You could see my knickers," she said. "It was so embarrassing."

Still, it could always have been a lot worse. With a coat on to cover her secret, she was able to dash home and change.

The job only lasted for the first few months of the band, until they winged their way over to England and really got down to business. But it did give her some experience of the real world, and the things she'd encounter there.

Now, of course, Lindsay lives the reality of the band, and her schedule is busier than anything she could imagine. That doesn't mean she's exempt from embarrassing situations, though. Like all the others, she has her share of moments she'd rather not remember—and just like the others, she gets teased about them.

"One night the lights went off when I was onstage and I fell off the back of the stage. Luckily the lights were off so I was saved the embarrassment of anyone seeing me." Still, there was a sore tush, and the rest of the girls knew what had gone on and weren't about to let Linds forget it quickly.

With all the traveling they do now, and very little free time, it's been a lot harder for Lindsay to see the people she cares about, particularly as her mother and father still live in different countries. Last December she managed a few days in Greece, luckily at the same time as her mother was visiting, but it's not easy to see either of her parents.

"The only drawback about this job is being away from friends and family for a long time."

On those rare occasions that she has a little free time, if

Lindsay isn't in Dublin, the chances are you'd be able to locate her in Athens.

"I always love going back to Greece, where I was born," she explained. "I don't get to go as often as I'd like, which is quite sad. The best time of year to go there is in the spring, when all the countryside comes alive with the prettiest wild flowers. I really miss it, actually." Given the opportunity for her dream vacation, she'd be literally flying all over the world. She'd begin with a couple of days in Greece, then move on to Mauritius (" 'cause I've heard it's beautiful"). From there it would be an extreme change of climate, all the way north to Alaska, then back to the sunshine, to finish in the Caribbean. It actually sounds more exhausting than relaxing!

Of course, Linds has to work a lot harder as a member of B*Witched than she would have done as a student—and there's also a lot less vacation time. But she wouldn't trade the two things for the world, even if she can't see too much of her family.

That's the down side. To look at things more positively, being part of a top band means she gets to mix with the people whose CDs she used to buy just a few short years ago. One item that's always in her carry-on is her portable CD player, along with a selection of albums by the Verve, Robbie Williams, 5ive, and All Saints—all of whom she's come to know on a personal level recently. It's a big change going from fan to equal, but that doesn't mean she'd be comfortable just walking up to every star. She can get a little tongue-tied, and if she were to meet one of the real superstars, she admits she probably wouldn't know how to carry on a conversation.

"I adore Mariah Carey's voice and would love to meet her, but if I ever did, I'd probably go all tongue-tied and just say, 'Oh hello. . . .' "

The same would probably be true if she were to run into either of her favorite movie stars, Meg Ryan and Brad Pitt

("I love everything about him"). In fact, one of her dreams is to co-star in an action movie herself.

"Something with loads of kick boxing," she fantasized. "It'd be great if Brad Pitt could co-star—he can rescue me anytime."

Given her Brad fixation, it might be surprising to learn that her all-time favorite film doesn't include him in any shape or form. In fact it's *Titanic*, "because it made me feel very emotional and I like Leo!" Going to see it at the theater probably wasn't the best idea for Lindsay, because "I cry very easily." and that was exactly what she did. "I was sobbing and shaking so much when I went to see *Titanic*, the whole cinema was staring!"

She also loves older films, so when they're all at home in Surrey, and the others are sitting around watching their soaps, Lindsay will be off doing something else, but she'll come back later and "stay up to watch a late film." When the time off happens, though, what she wants to do more than anything is "sleep!" That's understandable. Being on tour, or constantly in demand, jetting from one country to another, isn't very restful. That's the price of fame, and one Linds is willing to pay. Give her a few days off and she's ready to get going again, her batteries all recharged. To tell the truth, if she had a month to herself, she probably wouldn't know what to do with all the free time, although the girls would spend some of it going "to the cinema, maybe go bowling, listen to music. We like to just hang out together, we enjoy each other's company."

Until the band relocated to London, Lindsay had always worn her hair long. But a new country meant the chance to change her image, and Linds opted to have it cut shorter—it would be easier for dancing that way, too. She had visions of herself looking very glam and sophisticated, but in the end it didn't turn out exactly the way she'd hoped.

"I remember when I had my hair cut from long to short," she laughed. "The hairdresser got carried away and it ended up shorter than I'd planned. I looked like a boy.'' Of course, that's not how she looks now, since it grew back a long time ago, but at least it let her know that really short hair just wasn't her!

She's quite obsessive about her hair actually, and she always washes it twice, just to make sure it's completely clean—which means she takes longer in the bathroom than all the other girls. And she always uses her hair dryer, because ''without it, my hair just doesn't go right.'' On days off, though, it's a different matter altogether. ''If I'm not working I don't care what my hair looks like—I just stick a hat or gel on it! When we're working it takes four hours for us to have our hair and makeup done, 'cause there's only one makeup artist between us!'' Lindsay is also the one who'll get out the tweezers when they have a girlie night and do everybody's eyebrows, including her own, of course.

While she's obsessive about her hair, it also extends to other things. Creep into the room she shares with Edele at night, and you'll find her watch sitting on the dresser—''The tick is so loud, I can never sleep with it on.''

Along with the other girls, she's really not the party animal you might expect. They get invited to all the best parties, of course, but they rarely attend.

''We haven't been to one—honest,'' Linds said. ''What's the point, 'cause we always have to get up the next day and do about ten hours' work!'' And even if a girl is already beautiful, she needs her beauty sleep.

Apart from kick boxing and netball, Lindsay has never been the sporty type, and these days she gets her workouts when she performs. In the last couple of years, the farthest she's walked has been two miles. ''It was half a mile to the pier, then the pier was half a mile long, then I walked home again.'' Still she keeps in great shape, always swimming in the hotel pool if there is one. And she's one of those lucky people who doesn't have to watch what she eats. She can get away with drinking regular milk, which is probably just as well, as she hates the taste of skim milk. "Semi-skimmed just doesn't taste like milk," she said firmly. And that extends to food, too. She really enjoys "good Irish chicken stew and potatoes. I love boiled potatoes. Over in America, they think you're mad if you ask for boiled potatoes." Chicken (as well as potatoes) is a big part of her diet, since she, like Edele, doesn't eat any red meat. So by now she's sampled almost every chicken dish hotel kitchens and promoters can come up with. While she prefers home-cooked food from the cook they take along with them, that's not always possible, so it's just as well she hasn't got sick of chicken yet!

Needless to say, living on top of the others all the time, there are little things about Lindsay that can annoy the others. She herself admits that "I get impatient with people," but that's not what gets to the other girls. It's her ... slippers. "Apparently they're really noisy," she laughed. But the girls are like family to each other, not just out of necessity, but out of genuine friendship.

Their denim, tomboy image has become inextricably associated with them now, but it's Lindsay who's really taken it to extremes. She once attended a friend's wedding wearing ... denim! As it turned out, it wasn't deliberate. She'd fully intended on getting dressed up. But the case with the clothes she wanted to wear had gotten lost, just leaving her the choice of denim or denim. And so she chose denim. But it wasn't a complete disaster. Everyone understood. Luckily she has some good friends.

Good friends are a plus, but there are times they can also seem like a minus. Whenever Lindsay makes it back to Ireland, they all want to see her as soon as she's reached her mum's house.

"They call us as soon as they know we're home," she said, "and want us to go out, but we always get home awfully tired." She's as up for a laugh and a good time with her mates as anyone else, but she also needs her time to chill a little first, and visit with her family.

* * *

When it comes to the blokes, Lindsay just doesn't have the time or the opportunity for a relationship at the moment, but that doesn't mean she won't flirt a little—or a lot, depending on who she's with.

"I can be a bit of a flirt," she admitted. "I make loads of eye contact, smile and mess about in a jokey way. I don't believe in chat up lines, though—I crack jokes instead."

And in the past she's been egged on by her friends to approach boys she liked,

"I did a 'drink and dial' once—you know, when you've had a few and you think it's a really good idea to phone that person you fancy and tell them exactly how you feel. I'm not saying who it was, but I'm glad his mother answered and he wasn't at home because it could've been really embarrassing!"

When it comes to something serious, though, it's a different matter. "I don't know who my ideal man would be. He'd have to have a great personality and everything." If push were to come to shove (and if he asked), she'd probably marry Brad Pitt. "I know everyone likes him, but he *is* lovely!"

One thing you won't find Lindsay near is sharks. "I've hated them ever since I saw the movie *Jaws*," she said, and one time she got closer to them than she'd planned. The girls were in Hong Kong, and in some free time, Lindsay decided to go swimming in the sea. Hong Kong has sharks, and to protect swimmers, they have shark nets strung in the water in the bay. Lindsay got totally freaked when she realized she'd swum *past* the nets, and could possibly become an hors' d oeuvre for some teeth and fins. She swam back to safety faster than she'd ever moved in her life!

Just like Edele, Lindsay likes her teddy bears. Their room is almost a shrine to teddies—they're everywhere, and simply moving them so they can get into their beds is a major operation. But to Lindsay, as well as Edele, each one has a meaning, and she'd never part with a single one of them.

One thing they've never seen in the bedroom, or anywhere else in the house for that matter, is a ghost. Lindsay doesn't really believe that the place is haunted, but she's certain that somewhere, somehow, ghosts are completely real.

"Just because I've not experienced one doesn't mean they don't exist," she insisted. For Lindsay, the truth is most definitely out there. She might believe in ghosts, but she has a lot more difficulty believing in herself as a celebrity. To her, she's exactly the same old Lindsay she's always been. She hasn't changed a bit.

"I first realized I was a pop star when we heard we were Number One. I suppose that makes you a pop star. I still can't think of myself as a pop star, though—it's weird! *You* don't change, but the things around you do."

And they change very quickly. These days Lindsay is used to flying first-class, and being met at the airport by a driver. But it's not that long since the only limo she'd ever been in was for her school graduation party. Times change!

One thing doesn't change, however: Lindsay still has her feet firmly planted on the ground. Of course, the other girls wouldn't let her get carried away with the fame business, but even from within it's still Lindsay the girl, not Lindsay the celeb. Her mother reinforces that, too. Having a couple of free days, Linds decided to make a quick trip to Ireland to see her mum. Unfortunately, she'd left the key to the Irish house in Surrey. She arrived late, when her mother was already in bed, and had to ring the bell to be let in. Instead of being happy to see her daughter, Sharon told her off for arriving so late and scaring her with a midnight knock on the door! No way is that girl ever going to get a swelled head! That becomes particularly true when she sees the effect B*Witched's music and presence can have on others.

"We were doing a photo shoot one day and this little

girl that had leukemia came in," Lindsay recalled. "She won a competition to meet us and her little face just lit up. And just to see that... and her mother was saying, 'You really have made her day.' And if we could have that happen, that has to be magical." It also puts things into a very clear perspective. If Lindsay can do something that touches someone so deeply, someone whose problems are so much greater than most of us face, it all becomes worthwhile, and means far more than all the Number Ones. Much the same thing occurs when she has a chance to look at the mail the band gets.

"We get letters and stuff from people saying, 'When I feel sad or depressed, listening to your music makes me feel better.' " Reading things like that give more satisfaction than anything, hearing directly from the people she's touched along the way. It's not all about money (although, let's face it, a little bit helps), it's about reaching people emotionally. And obviously the girls do that very well.

At five foot five, Lindsay is the smallest of the girls, and weighs in around one hundred and twenty pounds, and, given that she's always in denim, it's probably quite handy that her favorite color is blue—"navy blue, electric blue, and baby blue." She's a person who takes the present as it comes—well, things have happened in such a rush, there's barely been time to consider the future. She's living the dream she's had since childhood, and that certainly can't be bad. It's all she ever wanted. Ask her what she'll be doing in the year 2009, though, and things become a bit more confused.

"I don't know what I'll be doing in ten years, but hopefully I'll be married. I definitely see myself singing and being in the record business."

In all likelihood she will be. Having achieved your dream, why would you want to let it go, especially when it's turned out to be everything you hoped—and you've made three best friends doing it! Hopefully, in ten years

Lindsay will have a house of her own that she can fill with all the cats she loves.

Mostly, however, if she had one wish: "I think it would be for us to be happy. That kind of includes our friends and family being okay. If the people around us are [happy], we are happy."

When the girls first got together, it was all practice, practice, practice, and it was an exciting time for them all, particularly Lindsay, who was still in school and the real baby of the group. Nowadays there's very little rehearsal, because the girls are performing almost every day, and are in top shape. That will probably change after the summer, however, as they prepare for the release of their second album and a headlining U.K. tour in November. There'll be an entirely new act, and maybe even a new image. Before "C'est La Vie" appeared, Lindsay had wanted hair that was kind of different—both curly and straight—but everyone agreed that one or the other seemed better. Perhaps this time they'll let her have her way. It's also just possible that the girls will get rid of all the denim and begin wearing something else (although you might not want to hold your breath on that one).

There may not be much free time, but Lindsay does enjoy some of the perks of fame. Apart from the travel, there's also the unexpected free meal. "We went out for a Chinese meal one night and because we gave the staff autographs for all their kids we didn't have to pay!" In Britain and Ireland, everyone knows their faces, but Linds isn't going to complain—after all, it's what she wanted. "It is getting to the stage where we can't do everything we want to," she admitted. "Some stars say it's not fair having no privacy, but how lucky are they doing the job they do?" Even if it's much harder work (and much less glamorous) than she'd expected, Lindsay isn't about to walk away from all this. She's having the time of her life with her three closest friends, singing and dancing, and having her album bought by millions of people. It's probably just as well now that she turned down college to follow her heart.

Sometimes life really can turn out just the way you'd hoped it would. In Lindsay's case, it's certainly happened. The secret seems to be not to let your dreams down in everyday realities. Hold them tight, do everything you can to pursue them, and good things really can happen—they did for Linds!

"Even if it all ended tomorrow I'd be happy," she said. "I just take each day as it comes and am thankful for what we've achieved."

Keavy

B*WITCHED MAY NOT BE about Girl Power and feminism the way the Spice Girls are, but in her own quiet way Keavy does a lot to further the cause of women everywhere. Not only is she a member of a top band, but she can also kick box, tootle on a saxophone, dance, do gymnastics *and* she can fix your car. Now that's what you call a well-rounded person.

Keavy-Jane Elizabeth Annie Lynch (which is quite a mouthful, hence she's known as just Keavy or Keaves), is actually fractionally older than her twin sister, Edele. They both popped into the world on December 15, 1979, and, until Edele got her scar on their third birthday, it was virtually impossible to tell them apart. Even their parents, Brendan and Noeleen, had a difficult time.

When Edele was three, she got eighteen stitches, but Keavy had it even worse—that year she ended up in the hospital with pneumonia. She was the only kid on the ward who wasn't allowed out of bed, so while all the others were playing, she just had to lie there and watch, which made her feel even worse!

B*Witched have a very tomboyish image, but if there's one person who exudes the tomboy factor, it's Keavy, and she's been that way since she was little. When other girls were playing with dolls, she was out playing games—physical education was always her favorite subject in school, and she won medals for gymnastics and swimming, as well as playing on the school volleyball team. Her love of physical activity was apparent from an early age.

"The last white Christmas we had was when I was about six," she recalled. "We have a van, and when the roads were icy, our dad used to attach tires, rocking horses, and bits of cardboard to the back. Then we'd sit on them and go flying around the roads." It was dangerous, but she loved every second of it.

Being identical twins, Keavy and Edele have always been very close, sharing a special bond that seems almost telepathic at times. Even now, they'll still occasionally say the exact same thing at the same time—kind of spooky, really. But while Edele loves to talk, Keavy has always been shyer and a bit more retiring. When their older sisters, Tara and Alison, first brought Edele and Keavy to school, Edele immediately settled down with the other girls. But Keavy just cried and cried when her sisters left. Once she settled into the routine, however, she started making good grades—at least until her transition year, when she became bored and acted up a bit in class.

In every class except P.E., anyway. That she always loved. Any excuse to be active, running, playing, to do some kind of sport and be energetic suited her perfectly. And that was why dance suited her so perfectly. It had always been something she'd done. "My brother and I would sing and dance a lot at home and put on little shows. There were six of us and we totally loved to entertain."

Edele had been studying dance for a couple of years, but Keavy didn't begin lessons until she was thirteen, going down to Digges Lane, although she little suspected it would become so important in her future. In fact, she was late for her very first lesson because she wanted to make sure she had the right shoes and pants. Keavy and her parents had to run all over Dublin to find them, only to get there and discover she was the only one properly dressed anyway!

Being very physical and coordinated, Keavy proved to

be a natural dancer. She started out studying jazz dance, but quickly, along with Edele, also started learning hip-hop. That was a lot more complex, but the two girls quickly got the hang of it, and with Edele's ambition pushing them, they formed a hip-hop dance group with their friends Mark, Danny, Graham, and Peggie-Anne. Before they knew what was happening they were in demand for all manner of promotional events, hired by the likes of Coca-Cola, and also Sony for their big Irish launch of PlayStation.

While all this was great fun, it was very far from the dream Keavy had when she was a little girl. Back then, her big ambition in life was to be a fireman. (She really was a tomboy! But in the modern world, why shouldn't she be anything she wanted to be?) Actually, it's still not that far from her mind, although she jokes that "I suppose I'd have to do it part-time if I did it now."

One secret that Keavy has is that she was once a calendar girl. No, it wasn't one of *those* calendars. She was seven years old at the time, and it was for a vacation resort in Britain. Her parents entered a picture of Keavy on a train in a competition, and she proved to be one of the winners. That was her first taste of fame, although no one except her family ever recognized her.

If you ever get a chance to see Keavy's hands up close, you might well notice that one of her fingers is bent. It all happened when she was young. Cars had always fascinated her, and she'd hang around when her father was working on them at his garage. One day she and Edele were messing around, and Edele accidentally shut a car door on Keavy's finger. Of course, Keavy was yelling with pain, and it really hurt, but once she was free it didn't seem too bad, and she didn't want to go to the hospital. Looking back, she said, "I think it broke, but I never had it fixed, so now it's bent."

Like her twin, Keavy inherited the family's musical talent, and as a teenager she joined a band called the Dublin Allstars. This certainly wasn't a B*Witched type band—in fact, it couldn't have been further away. This was a marching band. While Edéle played the flute, Keavy played the alto saxophone and also doubled as a majorette, twirling a flag. It was a great honor for them both when the band was invited to New York to take part in a St. Patrick's Day parade, and their first trip away from home without their parents. Needless to say, Keavy wasn't too tomboyish on that trip!

That was the exception more than the rule, though. She was happiest being one of the lads, never really caring what she wore. One summer she and a friend were out on the River Liffey in Dublin on her dad's boat. They were hungry, so they moored and walked up to McDonald's for lunch—still in their wetsuits, dripping river water all over the place. Keavy didn't care how she looked.

She was shy with new people, but always willing to try new things. So when some of her male friends got tattoos, she wanted one too. She knew her parents would object, so she sneaked out one day and had one done, a small one on her left shoulder, the Chinese symbol for happiness. Then she started to panic. She couldn't let her folks see it. So, for over a year she managed to keep it hidden from them, until the day finally came when she forgot, and they noticed it. In her mind, she'd thought it would cause this huge commotion, but they proved to be not all that bothered.

And having had a tattoo, she also decided to have a piercing—and decided to go for one of the most obvious of all, her tongue. "It didn't really hurt," she said. "My mobile [phone] rang when I was getting it done, so I ended up giggling! But I had to eat soup for ages afterwards, so I took it out." Giggling has always been a trait of hers when she's not at ease. "I do it when I'm nervous," she explained, wishing she could stop. "I giggle and everyone stares, so I giggle even more. I hate it."

Keavy wasn't particularly interested in any kind of an academic career. She seemed to be happiest when she was busy doing something, rather than sitting in a classroom learning—all part of that energy she still has. In that regard, she was like Edele, and her parents knew better than to try and persuade them to stay in school, where they wouldn't be happy. It would be better for them to leave when they were sixteen, and discover what they really wanted to do.

For Edele that seemed to be dancing, and Keavy loved working with BOOM and Starlight, along with her sister. And, like her twin, Keavy loved to sing. She'd sing along with anything and dance around in her room at home.

It was more natural for the girls to think about forming a band than for most, since their big brother was finding huge amounts of success with *his* band. Boyzone seemed unstoppable (and, indeed, they've just enjoyed their sixth British Number One, keeping former Spice Girl Geri Halliwell out of the top singles slot). They never exactly sat down and talked to Shane about it all. Instead, they could see what he did, how hard he worked, and what was necessary to be successful. He had drive and ambition, and neither of them was short of that. When pressed to name her favorite groups, Keavy will still say Boyzone first, even though she admitted, "I know that's naff 'cause Shane's my brother." But family has always been more important than anything else.

The odds of lightning striking twice, and of the twins putting something together that could be as successful as Boyzone were small, and they realized it. Still, it was a thought that remained at the back of Keavy's mind. It would be the perfect way to make a living, she thought as she worked in Stadium Sports (yes, the same place as her sister!). Unlike Edele, she didn't stay in retail for too long. It simply wasn't her; there wasn't enough activity about it. She was looking around for something new when her father casually mentioned one evening that he was looking for a trainee mechanic.

He and Noeleen had always told the girls they could be whatever they wanted to be, but it was still a shock when Keavy asked if she could have the mechanic's job. After all, that was traditionally men's work. But Keavy had always been the real tomboy, and he had to admit that cars and engines had always interested her. At the same time, he wanted someone who would work hard and learn, not get bored and leave after just a few weeks.

Keavy was dead serious, though. While it might never have occurred to her as a career before, the more she thought about it, the more she liked it. She continued to press her dad, and after a short time he gave in and agreed to take her on. The work was very physical, but that didn't bother her a bit; in fact she loved it. Even starting out on the very basics, like changing tires and doing oil changes, was great fun, and she loved it when she'd roll out from under a car and people would be astonished to see a girl. Without even trying, she was doing her bit for the feminist movement in Ireland. It wasn't without its ups and downs, however.

"A man said I put petrol in his car instead of diesel. I didn't, but I was so nervous I just laughed and laughed." Which didn't sit too with either the man or her father when he came out to see what was happening.

It was at this time she took up kick boxing, just because it seemed appealing. She was still dancing with Edele, and between everything, she had very little free time. She quickly rose through the kick boxing ranks, all the way to a blue belt, and her instructor, Martin Farrell, tried to persuade her to compete. For Keavy, there was a big difference between learning the techniques as exercise and for self-defense and actually going in the ring to hurt someone. She didn't want to do that, and refused to take part in any tournaments. And, of course, it was in Farrell's kick boxing class that she first met Lindsay. That would prove to be every bit as fateful as the first time she began chatting to Sinead, at her dad's garage.

In many ways, Keavy was the person who put the band together. She was certainly the central point for it all, the only one who knew everyone concerned. And she couldn't be happier that it's all worked out.

While she'll never be a fully qualified mechanic now, that doesn't stop her helping out her dad on those rare occasions she's at home. In part, it's because it gives her a chance to spend some time with him, but also because she just enjoys doing the physical work—it makes a complete change from being on the stage every night! It just goes to show, you can make the girl into a star, but you can never take the tomboy out of her.

That tomboy extends to her wardrobe. The B*Witched image is all denim, but Keavy has taken it far more to heart than all the others. She owns fifteen pairs of denims—in fact, it's pretty much the only way she dresses, and always has been. And just in case you wondered, underneath she wears Calvin Klein's "because they're so comfortable!" No sexy lingerie for her! You might well call her the inspiration for the band's look. Her look is completely natural. There's very rarely dye in her hair, and she doesn't often use perfume; in fact, the only one she'll ever wear is Dune by Christian Dior, because "it's the only scent that doesn't smell like hairspray to me." No fancy shampoos or soaps for Keavy ("I don't really use soap—I use shower gel instead."). Her biggest beauty treatment is trying to get as much sleep as she can. "To be wide awake in the morning, I need about eight hours," she admitted. Maybe her biggest concession to beauty was the fact that "I wore braces when I was about sixteen—train tracks. The thought of getting 'em bothered me, but when the time came to take them off, I was like, 'No, I don't want to. Put them back on!'" She does have one slightly curious dream about her looks, though. "I'd like to have purple hair for a day—and a tan. That might look a bit odd, but never mind!" Why purple? Well, because it just happens to be her favorite color. She doesn't wear contacts, but she'd still like to have a pair of purple contact lenses, just because!

Her biggest vice, such as it is, is talking on the phone. And that means talking a *lot*. When the girls are at home in Surrey, they all agree that between seven and midnight it's almost impossible to pull Keavy away from the receiver. And if she's not talking on that phone, you can find her out and about chatting merrily away on her cell phone—her bills are quite regularly about $600 a month! It's become a joke, not only in the band, but all over Britain, the amount of time Keavy spends talking on the phone, but she takes it in good part, mostly because she knows it would be impossible to deny. Needless to say that, along with her Wrigley's Doublemint gum, the one thing she makes sure to have in her purse is her cell phone—she'd be totally lost without it.

Even though she's a huge star nowadays, underneath it all she's still the same shy Keavy she's always been, not too comfortable around strangers. She does try to hide it a little—meeting strangers all the time is part of being a pop star—but she knows what she's really like.

"I've been called cute and giddy, but I think I'm more shy because I never know what to say to new people," she explained. And this constant barrage of new folk makes her worst habit even worse. When she's thinking or she's nervous, Keavy tends to bite the inside of her cheek. On press days or on tour, it tends to be almost raw!

Still she has her closest friends by her side, including here "bestest friend," Edele. The two remain remarkably close, although they don't room together in the Surrey house. Keavy actually shares with Lindsay, in the room that doesn't even have a wardrobe, just a rail for their clothes, as well as a wax hand sitting on the dresser. It's actually Keavy's hand—or at least a wax impression of it, that she had made in a shop in Blackpool, the English seaside resort, when the girls were appearing there. While Keavy and Sinead don't have as many stuffed animals on their beds as Edele and Lindsay, there are still quite a few that end up on the floor every night. If you're outside the house at night, you'll be able to tell which is Keavy and Lindsay's room—it'll be the one with the light on. Keavy still hates the dark, and always sleeps with a light on. It doesn't bother

her, or stop her getting those eight hours (and it obviously doesn't bother Lindsay, either!)

Like the other girls, Keavy takes her turn at cooking when they're in Surrey. But if she's going to make you a meal, you'd better be prepared for something with chicken in it—it's her favorite food. If it has chicken, the chances are that Keavy can cook it! When she's going to snack, though, she doesn't immediately turn to something sweet. Keavy actually prefers her chocolate plain, rather than milk (odd, since she loves to drink milk), "because it's yummy and leaves a great taste in your mouth."

She loves to watch her soaps, but one thing you'll never find Keavy glued to when the television's on is soccer. It may be the biggest sport in the world—and certainly the most popular in the U.K.—but she couldn't care less about it.

One thing she certainly does care about is her family. Nothing means more to her in the world than her parents, her brother, and her sister. She's proud of them all, in exactly the same way they're proud of her. "I'm really protective of my family," she said. "It's never happened, but if I heard anyone saying anything bad about them, I'd just go mad!" In fact, much of that massive monthly phone bill of hers comes from talking to members of her family. "I always get tearful when I think how far away from our family we are. I sometimes cry when I'm on the phone to my parents. I'm glad the others are there to make me feel better!" Given that Keavy is a real tomboy, it's not surprising that she's especially close to her dad, and he once, jokingly, gave her some advice she still recalls: "Me dad always told me that if someone slags you off, you should slag them back. If someone pushes you, you push them back. And if anyone hits you, you absolutely murder them. Hahahaha!"

Being the gentle soul that she is, none of that would ever happen to Keavy—particularly since she has that blue belt in kick boxing. Still, best not to make her mad and find out, eh?

Along with her love of her family, Keavy is totally committed to the band and the music they make. "We totally believe in the power of pop music to raise people's spirits," she said, and that's not just hype. These are girls who co-write most of their own material, and they've seen the effect it can have—an effect which is completely, er, bewitching. "Putting a smile on someone's face with your music is just magic!" Keavy added, and she understands that the name B*Witched really does have a deeper significance, as if this is what they were all put on the earth to do. "I believe the things that happen to you happen for a reason. Everybody's different and that's the beauty of the world." Together, as a unit, these four girls really have made a difference in people's lives, have made them happier for a little while—and that's no small accomplishment. Maybe it's only pop music, but that can be powerful enough. And they've seen that somehow the band is more than the sum of its four parts. There's a bond between Keavy and the others that will always be unbreakable, no matter what happens. "We'll always be B*Witched," she said. "Even when we're in our forties! We've experienced something together that no one can ever take away from us." Not that anyone would want to. And there's a lot more still to come, so many great things ahead of them yet. She's a little star, isn't she? Maybe that's why for her B*Witched ring, Keavy chose the magical star symbol. It really does mean something to her.

When the band does get criticism, she's the one who tends to take it all to heart. Perhaps because she's the shyest, she's also the most sensitive, with the thinnest skin. The others can laugh things off, but they stay with Keavy. She thinks and broods about them, and ends up taking them to heart—which is not always a good thing. In a way, it goes hand in hand with her romantic side. Yes, although she's still very much the tomboy, she's enough of a girlie to be romantic and love a good, weepy movie. Her favorite, in fact, is *Sleepless in Seattle*, simply "because it's so romantic."

That even applies to a lot of the music she enjoys. There's Boyzone of course, which she'd like even if it weren't for the family connection, because they specialize in romantic ballads. And there's Savage Garden, whose "Truly, Madly, Deeply," was a huge romantic hit. When she wants to get more dance-y, Keavy puts on Janet Jackson, and you can never go wrong with Janet if you want to move around.

Like the others, she's not much of a party girl. In fact, the lasses in B*Witched are probably about as clean-living as you're going to find anywhere. Granted, there's no time for anything else, but there's not the inclination, either.

"People say we must have some skeletons in the closet, but we don't!" she protested. "People can dig deep, but they'll never find anything," she joked, "apart from Sinead was expelled from school on her last day, but how would you find that out?" And, as if to prove they really were good girls, she recounted an incident that happened when they were in the U.S. "There was this club in New Orleans, and all the guys were wearing strings of beads around their necks. For the girls to earn their beads they had to pull up their tops and flash their boobs! Can I just say, by the end of the evening, we didn't have a single necklace on us." So Keavy and the others aren't the wild girls. But there have been a couple of instances when she's done a no-no. For example, there was the time she stole a hotel towel—not exactly the crime of the century. The girls had been using it to wipe off hair dye, and it was completely ruined. Keavy, embarrassed, tossed it into her suitcase rather than give the hotel a useless towel back. And obviously she's immune to the idea of seven years' bad luck for breaking a mirror. She did it once it a hotel in Amsterdam—knocked it over and watched it snap in half. It was a complete accident, of course, and she immediately expected the worst.

But everything has turned out fine . . . so far. Well, they do tell you to watch out for the shy ones.

When it comes to the guys, Keavy has very definite tastes. If she's ever in the same room as Mel Gibson, you'd better get out of the way. He's her dream man—"He's funny and more than a bit *pwhorrgh!*" Now, while he might seem a bit old for her, that's okay—Keavy tends to go for the older ones, finding boys her own age "too immature." One thing she's definitely not is stuck-up; when it comes to romance she's not just going after the famous and rich. "I'd date the milkman if he was nice!" she said. The thing is, she truly means it—it's not what a guy does that's important, but what he's like. Having said that, though, Keavy isn't actively looking. "Sometimes I'd like to have a boyfriend," she admitted, "but I'm not looking for one because everyone knows if you look for a boyfriend, you'll never find one! If I happened to meet the right person, then great, but I'm quite happy on my own, thank you!" One thing she certainly isn't interested in is a guy who thinks that because she and Edele are twins, they're the same in every way—sort of interchangeable. "I hate it when they don't care which one of us they're with," she said firmly.

Besides, where would she find the time for a boyfriend? But if you think you know the perfect bloke for Keavy, don't set her up on a blind dinner date. The idea just creeps her out. She could never sit down for a dinner for two with someone she's never met before. "People find that weird," she admitted. "They say, 'Of course you could!' But I just can't." See, she really is shy!

Just like the other girls, what you see with Keavy is exactly what you get. No airs and graces, no snobby attitude now that she's a big star. She's exactly the same girl, the one who can pop home for a few days and be found working at her dad's garage, just to keep her hand in and be real. No fancy frocks in her closet—or on the rail in her bedroom, anyway—and she doesn't have tons of makeup in the bathroom cabinet. Put her in a pair of jeans and a T-shirt, and she's completely happy. Of all of them, she's most definitely the most tomboyish. But she loves what she's doing, the singing and dancing, and making people happy. It's given her opportunities to see places she'd never have gone otherwise, and even she couldn't resist shopping on Rodeo Drive in L.A. when they were filming their *In Concert* for Disney, or when they made a publicity trip to New York, which was "absolutely fantastic. It's so busy and exciting and has got loads of fantastic shops—we went totally mad there!" So under the tomboy there really is a girlie trying to get out!

The last couple of years have been a whirlwind for Keaves. Constantly on the go, and often she's had to give up some of that eight hours' sleep she treasures. But she knows every sacrifice has been worthwhile. And even if B*Witched hadn't made it, she'd have still been in there, trying with something else. She seems laid-back, but she's also quite determined to succeed in whatever she attempts. And why shouldn't she be? "You only live once, so go for it and live life to the full!" she said, and that's exactly what's she been doing, and what she'd advise everyone else to do. If you don't pursue your dreams when you can, later in life you'll always wonder 'What if . . . ?" and that's not the most satisfying feeling in the world. If you fail, at least you tried.

Of course, Keavy wants to continue being successful, and to be happy. Who doesn't? And the chances are that she will. She's happy within herself, which is where it really counts, and any definition of success is always personal. She's accomplished a great deal, and B*Witched are poised to be one of the top groups of the millennium. They're young enough, eager enough, and energetic enough. She has everything going for her, and she's already at the top. Of course, all that fame does have a few drawbacks.

"We can't pop out to the shops, because in the last

house we lived people saw us going out for milk and started banging on the door all day!" As long as it's not overwhelming, and doesn't really invade her privacy, Keavy doesn't mind, though. After all, without the fans, they wouldn't have sold millions of records, and she knows that all too well. The fans may love them, but the girls owe the fans a debt, too. It's very much a two-way street. And being prepared for the fans is far more important than hanging out with other celebrities. Once, right after "C'est La Vie" had hit Number One in Britain, their record company took the girls out to dinner at Planet Hollywood. Did they make a big night of it, go out clubbing afterwards? Not a chance. Once ten-thirty rolled around, they were on their way home, to get enough sleep and prepare for the next day. They're professionals, and they have their priorities in order. They've rubbed shoulders with a lot of big names, including Celine Dion and the Bee Gees, and the only ones that have impressed these four girls are the ones who've remained real. Just like Keavy, Lindsay, Edele, and Sinead.

Somehow, in among all those different personalities, all the quirks and foibles, there's something that works just right. Something that keeps the girls together like family. That means they rarely fight, and treat each other like best friends. Call it magic, if you like, because magic is certainly what they seem to conjure up together.

One thing to always remember about B*Witched is that they're *Irish* girls (okay, apart from Lindsay, who's half-Irish, but who spent part of her life growing up there), and that means they were all brought up with Irish values. Their families will always be the most important thing in their lives, far bigger than any kind of material success. It's a value system that's not superficial, that sticks more to the old ways, but there's absolutely nothing wrong with that. It means that they don't take everything at face value, and they're not caught in the glitter and glamour of the star trap, like so many who become successful so quickly. They all have their feet very firmly planted on the ground—and, in their hearts at least, that ground is on the Emerald Isle. They know where they're going, but even more importantly, they remember where they came from. For Edele and Keavy, it's a lesson they've learned from their brother, Shane, and his experience in Boyzone. But even without that, it would have been the most natural thing in the world, as it is for Sinead and Lindsay.

It hasn't been a case of them all suddenly deciding to be pop stars and doing whatever they had to in order to make it happen. If anything, the stardom happened by a series of lucky accidents. Before that, though, they'd all put in years of work in different fields. They'd all persisted in their dreams.

What they've achieved, no one can ever take away from them. They have the gold records, the platinum records, collected from all over the world to stand as a testimony to B*Witched. And, the way they see it, they've only just begun; everything happened so quickly.

To hear them talk and laugh together is to know that these four girls are completely real. They couldn't be phony if they were paid a fortune; they wouldn't know how. This isn't a band that was manufactured by a manager to create hits. Instead, they're a genuine—in every sense of the word—phenomenon. They're modest, lovely, and above all, they're happy. They love the life they're living, and they're living the life they love. And, really, who can ask for more?

PART TWO

The Band

The Beginning 6

By now the story of B*Witched getting together has almost become the stuff of legend. It's one of those perfect little coincidences, and the kind of thing that couldn't have happened if Dublin wasn't a small town at heart, where people who moved in the same circles all knew each other, even if it was only to say hello.

Edele and Keavy both danced. They had a disco-dancing team called Starlight, and a hip-hop dancing team called BOOM, both of which were doing quite well about town. Both troupes trained at Digges Lane Dance Centre, where Edele and Keavy also taught dance classes. Still, they both harbored dreams of singing. However, they'd never received the kick they needed to do anything about it. Edele was working retail, and Keavy was training as a mechanic in their father's garage. Keavy was also taking kick boxing classes.

Sinead was a trained dancer, one who'd gone to dance school in England on a scholarship, before returning to Ireland to try her luck there. She had a flat in Dublin, and had been getting some small parts as a dancer, although not enough to support herself, which was why she was working as a cinema attendant. She, too, went to Digges Lane to practice, and vaguely knew the twins from there.

Lindsay was in her last year of high school. She'd done well on her Leaving Certificate, and had already been accepted at Trinity College in Dublin, where she planned to study business. But if there was one thing she'd always wanted, it was to be a pop singer. She had plans to record some demos and see what happened, but for the moment, those were just vague plans. For fun she'd taken up kick boxing the year before, which was where she'd met Keavy, and the two of them discovered the same ambition in life.

If Sinead's mother hadn't been having problems with her car, B*Witched might never have happened. Sinead had the day off, and she and Barbara, her mum, were out when the automobile started overheating. She did what anyone would—she pulled into the first garage she saw. By a stroke of fate—and what else could it have been—the garage was owned by Brendan Lynch, and Keavy was working there.

While the O'Carrolls waited for their car to be fixed, Sinead and Keavy began to chat. Their faces were familiar to each other from Digges Lane, but they'd never really stopped to chat before. Apart from the obvious talk about dancing, they began to talk about what they'd really like to do, and in both cases it was be part of a band.

Now, a lot of people want to join bands, but for most of them it's nothing more than idle talk, just daydreaming. If everyone who talked about forming a band actually put one together, the world would be inundated. But Keavy and Sinead were both serious. It helped that Keavy and Edele's older brother, Shane, was a member of one of Ireland's top bands, Boyzone, who scored plenty of hits, both in Ireland and the U.K. Keavy knew all too well what was involved, and the idea of hard work, rejection, and perseverance didn't worry her. And she knew her sister felt exactly the same way.

Even as they stood there, Sinead and Keavy started hatching the seeds of a band, even though it didn't have a name yet. There were the two of them, Edele would be into it, and Keavy knew another girl who might fit in perfectly, someone she'd met at kick-boxing. They could all sing, and they all knew how to move well. In theory, at least, it all seemed perfect. All they had to do was put it into practice, and where better to try things out than the place they all knew very well—Digges Lane? They could start out by having a chat and see how they felt about each other.

No sooner had Sinead and her mum left than Keavy was on the phone to Edele and Lindsay, setting things up for that evening. The four of them would get together and see what happened. She was excited; for the first time, she felt as if her secret dreams might really come true.

That evening, the four of them met each other properly for the first time.

"We seemed to get along, musically and as friends," Sinead recalled. Truthfully, they all felt as if there was something special in the air, and that it was magic. Although it was Keavy who brought them all together, "we feel that if we hadn't met that way, we would've met some other way, like fate."

They were eager, and thrilled, and ready to get to work. They arranged to get together the very next evening, only this time they'd do more than talk. They were a band, and a band needed songs and dance routines. It was time to get to work on both! They pooled their money, and reserved one of the small studios at Digges Lane to begin writing and rehearsing. In one quick burst, everything was starting to happen!

That first evening dancing together became a second, then a third, then every evening as things fell into place in a way none of them could have imagined. They moved well together, and their song ideas seemed to mesh perfectly. Within a few days the four of them were virtually living at Sinead's apartment. It was somewhere they could get together in peace and work on new song ideas, singing them into Sinead's little tape recorder, then build them up from there.

In fact, it was there that they first had an inkling that other people might also be enjoying their music. The four of them were working on a new song they'd written (and no, it's not one that survived), singing their hearts out, when suddenly there was a knock on the door. Immediately, the girls thought it was the neighbors, complaining about the noise. Being good lasses, they were quite prepared to apologize, and promise to keep it down in future. "But when we got out in the hall," Sinead recalled, "they said that they just wanted to hear what we were doing. And they said that we could turn the music up because they thought it sounded good." That's the sort of praise aspiring bands don't usually get, and it served as great encouragement.

In their free time, they were also going to Digges Lane to work on dance movements—they could possibly have done it at Sinead's but that would have *really* been pushing relations with the neighbors. In fact, at first they practiced every moment they could, anywhere they could. They weren't shy about trying things out in public, even. Early one evening, they all got together in St. Stephen's Green, one of the most famous parks in Dublin, and began their dance routines. All they had with them to play their music was a personal stereo with a pair of battery operated speakers—not the kind of thing that was going to drown out the whole park. In fact it was so quiet that the girls could barely hear it, let alone anyone else. "You could see people stopping and thinking, 'Why are those girls dancing at no music?'" Keavy laughed.

They were eager to push things, but also in no hurry; they wanted things to develop naturally. The influences they brought to this were diverse enough to create something interesting. There was soul, pop, hip-hop, and traditional Irish music in the stew, and it needed to simmer.

The cooking time proved to be less than they knew, however. Fate definitely seemed to be working for the girls—who didn't even have a name for their band yet!

After just a couple of weeks together, they were very happy with the way things were moving along. They'd already written some songs they felt proud of, and their dancing talent meant they'd been able to come up with moves more complex than most vocal groups. But they all knew there was still a lot of work to be done, a lot of refinements to be made, before they were ready to take it all public and conquer the world, girl-style.

What they didn't know was that one evening, after they'd only been together a couple of weeks, a crew would be filming a documentary about Digges Lane while they were rehearsing in one of the studios there. Being television people, they couldn't resist shooting some footage of four lovely girls moving around. The lasses didn't mind that; hardly anyone would know who they were, anyway.

What shocked them was when the producer came up and started talking to them. He'd liked what he'd seen. It turned out that he also produced a show that aired every Saturday morning, all throughout Ireland, and he wanted the girls to perform on it—that weekend.

Of course they were overjoyed, but in a state of panic at the same time. The tapes they'd made of songs they'd written only had vocals—no backing instruments, no beat. They had to come up with something before the weekend!

Immediately they sat down and pooled their money. Between them, they didn't have enough to go into a studio. So it was time to go to their families. Here they'd been offered this amazing opportunity, and they didn't want it all to slip away for the want of a few pounds. Brendan and Noeleen Lynch came through, slipping the girls some cash which allowed them, on a Thursday evening, to go into the studio and record four of the songs they'd written. It was probably just as well that they could all play instruments as well as sing, otherwise they'd have had no chance. Of the four tunes they put on tape, they picked "A Shoulder to Cry On" for their television debut.

They still needed a name, of course, and hurriedly came up with D'Zire. Okay, so it wasn't the best band name ever, but time was running short, and it did have a meaning— they were doing something they'd all desired to do. On top of that, they needed clothes, which involved frantically rushing around the shops, searching for something that might do. In the end, apart from matching boots—which cost over $150 a pair!—they settled for what they all had—denim.

The girls who looked very nervous (and who *were* incredibly nervous) on Irish television that Saturday morning didn't look a whole lot like the B*Witched of today. Yes, the denim was there, but the style was lacking. And Lindsay had blond hair with blue streaks—a far cry from her present black 'do. Obviously, they couldn't afford a stylist—they could hardly afford anything!

It was petrifying to be out there under the lights, performing to both the cameras and a studio audience, particularly as they'd only been together such a short time. But this was what they'd wanted, what they'd been aiming for; it had just come much sooner than they'd expected. So they gave it their all—what did they have to lose?

"A Shoulder to Cry On" wasn't the best song they'd ever write (which is why you've never heard it), but it was the best they had at the time. They were still learning, in every way, and improving all the time. And their performance was impressive. It was 1996, hardly anyone had heard of the Spice Girls yet, and a group of girls who sang and danced seemed like something new and completely fresh.

Certainly one viewer thought so. He called while the program—which went out live—was still on the air. And who was this mystery man? He just happened to be a tour promoter, and he was looking for an act to open for Boyzone on their next Irish tour. The call was patched through to the studio, where the girls were sitting, and they were asked if they wanted that opening slot. What else could they do but scream and answer, "Yes!"

For Edele and Keavy, it was a chance to spend some time on the road with their big brother (when the promoter called, he had no idea the two bands were related). The chances were coming their way as if this was just meant to be. But if they'd been panicking before their television appearance, now they were really scared. They didn't even have a proper act together yet, let alone a decent wardrobe. There was only one thing to do—they all quit their jobs, and threw themselves into two weeks of rehearsals before the tour started. It was exhausting, working ten and twelve hours a day on routines, trying to find time for some clothes shopping, but they had a goal now.

Life was suddenly more frantic than they'd ever thought possible, and they weren't even pop stars—yet! To go from nothing to opening a major tour in less than a month was like being caught in a whirlwind—they simply didn't know which way to turn. At least the first show wouldn't be in Dublin; they'd have a chance to get warmed up before they hit their hometown at the climax of the tour. Instead, the opening gig was in Belfast, north of the border, at the King's Hall. They'd only been in the crowd for gigs this size before, and peeking out, it seemed as if everyone in the city was there.

D'Zire, as they were still known, entered the stage in complete darkness, and waited for the music and the lights to come up. The music began, but somehow there was a glitch, and they were left to perform the first song in complete blackness, with the crowd not having a clue what was happening. The girls had no choice but to be complete troupers about it, and carry on as if that was what they'd intended all along. At first they were shaking so hard it was difficult to even keep hold of the microphones. Once the applause began, though, and they got into it, automatically remembering all the moves they'd worked on, they began to relax and really have fun. By the time their set was over, they felt as if they could have gone on all night.

The best part was the way they were received. Support acts usually get short shrift from an audience that's there to see the headliners. Everything else is just filling time, and at best, they're tolerated. But these four girls managed to win over the crowd with their songs, their moves, and their very natural friendliness. And that was the way it would be for the rest of the tour.

Even being on the tour was a dream come true, but there was more waiting for them. In the audience to check out D'Zire was a woman from England, Kim Glover. Along with her partner, Tommy J. Smith, she managed bands—in the past she'd done some work with New Kids on the Block. An Irish friend of hers had caught D'Zire on television, and phoned Kim to tell her about this hot new act. So she'd flown over to Belfast to judge for herself—and she was impressed with what she saw. They were raw, and needed a lot of work. But the potential was quite definitely there. After the show she came backstage and introduced herself to the girls. To them, just being on the tour was enough. It didn't seem as if things could improve, let alone improve so quickly.

Kim was definitely interested in managing the band, but she wanted to see more before she made any kind of decision. When the tour had finished, she flew to Dublin to meet the girls properly. Needless to say, the girls were nervous—getting management was big time! They took Kim down to Digges Lane, and ran through their set in one of the studios while she watched them. In fact, the girls were so nervous that they were unnatural, not even speaking unless they were spoken to. The next move was for her to bring over her partner. If he agreed, then they'd represent the girls. But if that happened, it would mean some major changes, the biggest of which would involve relocating to England. If they were going to get ahead in their careers, they needed to be at the center of the business—and that definitely wasn't Dublin.

One thing Kim suggested to the girls was to get as much experience as possible singing in front of audiences. It was something they were going to be doing a lot, and it would pay off in many ways. Their confidence would be increased, their act would become tighter, and they'd have a much better idea of what worked and what didn't. So

D'Zire began performing for schools around Dublin. It felt weird at first, given that none of them were long out of school themselves, but it was true—they did improve rapidly. They were also spending a lot of time at the dance studio, working as hard as they could to become a real class act.

When Kim returned with Tommy, she could see the changes. They were already one hundred percent better than they'd been in Belfast, full of enthusiasm and confidence, ready to take on the world and win. There was no doubt that this band could go places, and both Kim and Tommy wanted to be a part of it. Without any hesitation, they signed the girls to a management contract.

It was going to mean a lot of changes, and the biggest would be the move to London. Sinead, who'd spent a year there while learning dance, already knew the place, but none of the others had lived away from home before. Still, if they were going to make it—and they were determined to make it—there would have to be sacrifices. So Edele, Keavy, Lindsay, and Sinead packed up their stuff, said goodbye to their families, and boarded a plane at Shannon Airport. The future was just beginning.

Kim and Tommy had taken care of everything. They'd rented a house for the girls to live in. It wasn't in London, as it turned out, but in Surrey, just far enough away from the city to avoid any distractions, but still close enough to be easily accessible. There was no luxury of time to settle in and adjust to the new surroundings. No sooner had they unpacked than they were hard at work. There was a man Kim and Tommy wanted the band to meet, a producer called Ray Hedges, whom they thought might make an ideal partner for the girls. Hedges also had his own record label, Glow Worm, which had been set up as a independent through the major label, Epic, which was part of the massive Columbia group.

Ray Hedges had already achieved great success as a producer, notably with boy bands Bros and Boyzone (there was that connection again). He was very dubious about D'Zire, though. His experience was with boy bands, and he thought girls might be much harder to work with. But he couldn't deny they had talent.

"I was looking for something to break the mold, and they came to us with great songs," he said. "They're just Dublin rascals. They came over and Edele started singing and her voice was like Tammy Wynette meets Susanna Hoffs. They've all got really odd voices with no direct schooling." Edele, at least, was happy with the Susanna Hoffs comparison, since she'd always been a huge Bangles fan, and remembered singing "Eternal Flame" at the top of her voice when she was a kid. Once he heard and saw them, Hedges was convinced, even if it went against his better judgment. "I've waited a long time for my label, and the last thing I wanted to do was work with a girl band, but I signed them."

It was only for a production deal, not a record contract, but it was a huge leap for the girls. Like Kim, Hedges was convinced they had potential, and he was willing to work with them to develop it, which meant bringing the girls into his studio to help with the songwriting. He wasn't trying to take anything anyway from what they were doing, merely sharpen it all up.

Kim, too, was busy. The name D'Zire might have been fine when they were starting out—and it was one of those things they'd come up with on the spur of the moment—but, she thought, it just didn't sound or look as if it would play in the big leagues. So she suggested an alternative—Sassy. That seemed fine for a little while, until it was discovered that there was already a band with that name. Time for another change. So they came up with Sister. It wasn't the best, everyone knew, but it was the only one they could all agree upon.

Kim definitely wanted to push her charges. She could see them doing very well indeed. There were the writing sessions with Hedges, the work on the dance routines, and she thought they should also get used to dealing with the press. Which was why she sent them into London one day to visit *Live & Kicking* and *Top of the Pops* magazines.

It might have seemed premature—after all, no one in England had heard of them, and they didn't even have a record contract yet, let alone a record. But like good girls, they did what they were told, and visited the offices, full of good spirits, jumping around and singing songs from *The Sound of Music*, much to the amusement (and bemusement, probably) of the staff. To be sure, all the girls were nervous at the idea, and that translated into lots of energy, as if they were just bouncing off the walls. But there was no denying that they made an impression.

Pretty soon, however, they decided that they all hated the name Sister, and sat down with Kim and Ray Hedges to find something new. Suggestions were made, but they all seemed to fall flat, until Hedges piped up. He hadn't been eager to be involved with them at first, then "he said he thought we were very bewitching when we first met him," remembered Edele. "He kept saying it, and it just stuck!"

"We included the star in B*Witched because it made us sound a little different," added Lindsay. "We like the idea of our name to be a bit sparkly, so we put it in!"

Finally they had a name that everyone loved. It felt as if they'd reached a turning point. But they actually had much more than a name. They had a bunch of new songs, which they'd worked on with Ray. The next step was a deal—and that, too, came from Ray. After his initial reluctance, he'd become one of the band's biggest supporters, and now he singed them to a real record contract with his Glow Worm label. The next step was to have the girls perform for the executives at Epic (which financed Glow Worm), to try and get a development deal. That meant that Epic would give the girls a bunch of money to go away and write songs for several months. If the label liked what they heard, they'd release it. Being independent, Glow

Worm didn't have the money to offer them. It was the next step on the ladder, if you like. First, though, they had to audition for Ray Stringer, the managing director of Epic Records. That would be the real acid test. So far they'd won over everyone they'd come in contact with—could they do it once again?

The meeting had been set up for the private room of a fancy restaurant outside London, and Stringer no doubt thought that he'd be subjected to yet another girl group singing and trying to get signed. Certainly that's what the girls imagined he'd be thinking, which was why they decided *not* to sing. In fact, they set up something Stringer and his associates weren't about to forget in a hurry—a children's tea party. The table was heaped with bowls of Jell-O, sweets, ice cream, marshmallows, and candy. Not your standard audition—especially when the girls started a small food fight! The point, really, was to do something completely different, to jerk the suits out of their routine. And it worked.

"They remembered us, I can tell you!" laughed Lindsay. After Stringer left the restaurant, he called, and invited the girls to come down to the Epic offices on Great Marlborough Street and audition for him. It had paid off. Now he'd really listen to them.

On the day, the girls were on top form, running through some of the songs they'd written with Ray. Though none of them would end up making the cut for the album, they were much better than the material they'd been working on in Ireland. Ray had made some strong backing tracks, and it was undeniable that the lasses had *something*, a real streak of Irishness that ran through everything they did and made it fresh. Stringer, for one, was impressed, and offered the girls a development deal through Glow Worm. They'd have nine months to come up with enough good material for an album. If they succeeded, then the record would come out. If not ... well, they were too positive they'd succeed to think about that.

Now they were really off and running. The possibility of a single and an album was like a carrot dangling in front of them, and they wanted it badly. They buckled down to writing, spending every single day in the studio, getting up early and going home late in order to try and make everything absolutely perfect, to just blow the people at Epic away.

And from the start they were batting .1000. The first two songs they came up with were "C'est La Vie" and "To You I Belong." The latter was written for their parents, basically the sound of four girls away from home and missing their folks, a very lovely and personal ballad, and still one of their favorites. "C'est La Vie" (which is French for "that's life") was utterly different, upbeat and very bouncy.

"It's a song that could be interpreted a number of different ways," Edele said later. "But we see it as a kind of modern fairy tale—a song about being young and innocent. Which is pretty much how we feel at this time in our lives. We are writing songs from the view point of late teenagers. We're cheeky and we're giddy on life."

And they had every right to be. In just a few short months, their lives had completely changed. Giddy was hardly an adequate description. Euphoric was more like it; they were over the moon. They were loving every minute of their lives—well, how couldn't they? They were being paid to do exactly what they'd hoped to do, and the possibilities for the future were huge.

In its original form, "C'est La Vie" wasn't exactly the song that took the charts all over the world by storm. There was no Irish jig in the middle (that inspiration would come later), and the overall sound was more skeletal. But even then everyone knew there was something special about it, that it had hit written all over it. Stripped to the basics, it was still irresistible, and Ray knew, long before he'd had the go-ahead from Epic, that this would end up being the first single. He wanted to make it sound really special. Between him and the band, they came up with the idea of the Irish jig for the middle section.

It was a perfect idea. Not only did it emphasize B*Witched's Irish roots, it also tapped into the ongoing fascination with all things Celtic, like the global success of *Riverdance*. And, in the pop world, it would really stand out and get the track noticed and remembered—another hook. As if that wasn't enough, Sinead realized it would give the girls a chance to do some Irish step dancing—something she knew only too well, having studied it for years. That would give a ton of visual impact when they appeared live.

While they knew "C'est La Vie" was a total standout, they weren't pinning all their hopes on that. They wanted every song to be as good and as memorable. Everything had to be just right—the writing, arranging, the harmonies. What they wanted, essentially, was to present Epic with a record they not only couldn't refuse, but which would completely blow them away. It was hard work, but they didn't mind that one bit. This was what they'd been aiming for, and now they were so close they weren't going to fail for a little bit of effort. For five months they worked what seemed like every waking hour. They played and listened to songs over and over and over again, until they were sick of hearing them. Then they played them some more, because they weren't going to stop until they were satisfied.

Finally, five months into their development deal, they had what they believed was a great album. Ray, the seasoned professional, agreed—and if anyone would know, he would. They burned a CD of the tracks, sent it over to Epic, and began to wait nervously.

A few days later the girls had gone out for lunch. It was too stressful just sitting at home and waiting for the phone to ring. There was a café down the street where they could get something to eat and take their minds off the situation for an hour or so. They were joking around, waiting for the food to arrive, when Keavy's cell phone buzzed. That

1) The Cardiff Concert.

(Camerapress/Retna)

2) The ladies in denim.

(Melanie Edwards/Retna Ltd, USA)

3) Singing for the fans.

(David Wardle/Retna)

4) Performing in L.A.

(Steve Granitz/Retna Ltd.)

5) Always hyped for the show.

(Steve Granitz/Retna Ltd.)

6) The bewitching foursome.

(Colin Bell/Retna)

7) Hanging out and relaxing.

(Dave Hogan/All Action/Retna)

8) At the 1998 MTV Music Awards.

(Dave Hogan/All Action/Retna)

wasn't unusual—all her friends had the number and often called. She answered it, listened for a few seconds, and was suddenly wearing a huge smile. She hung up and turned to the others. It had been Rob Stringer from Epic on the line. He loved the tracks he'd heard, and Epic was definitely going to release their album! The girls began to hug each other, yelling and screaming. Every one of them was in floods of tears, completely overjoyed. They'd done it . . . they'd made it!

They were way too excited to eat now. They dashed home, making calls to Ireland, to Kim, to everyone they could think of. This was the biggest news any of them had ever had. Talking like mad they began making plans for the future. They were going to be huge; they really believed that. They weren't cocky or overconfident . . . it just seemed as if that was the way it had to be, as if fate was driving them forward.

That night they were still buzzed from the news. None of them could settle down and go to sleep. They stayed up late, simply savoring the news, daydreaming about the future, and thinking ahead to when the record would be in the stores and they could see it with their own eyes. Dreams really did come true, it seemed.

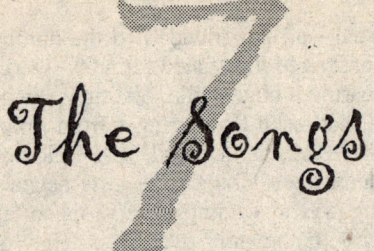

The Songs 7

THERE WAS STILL A LONG way to go before all that happened, though. First of all, before any record was issued, people had to know just who B*Witched were. That meant not only a press campaign, but also appearances around the country, live, on the radio, and on television. Also, it took time to gear up all the machinery.

And the album wouldn't be released quickly. First of all the company wanted to test the waters with a single, to see how that sold. As everyone had anticipated, they picked "C'est La vie," and the date for it to appear in stores as May, 1998. Of course, there was also a video to be shot—and that was where Sinead's dancing skills helped.

"She taught us the bit in the video," Keavy said. "Myself and Edele did a spot of Irish dancing when we were little and Lindsay had never done it before. Sinead was a good teacher, actually."

In a lot of ways that would be the highlight of the whole video, and of their live shows (for some concerts the band has a male dancer who joins them and mimes playing the fiddle, which is actually played by a member of their band).

With the video filmed, it was time to hit the road again. "It was mad," Keavy laughed. "We were so excited and it was great fun." Part of it was something they'd already done in Ireland—going to schools and performing, which they all enjoyed. "Meeting the kids who are going to buy your music is really nice," explained Sinead. "Sometimes they think you're unreal so it was great to get out there with them!"

Then, right before the single appeared, they started a U.K. tour, opening for top boy band 911. By now they were really professional, their routines elaborate and co-ordinated, the music filled out and energetic. They also had their image in place, all the denim from the same stores where everybody else shopped, with Edele emerging as the frontwoman to sing lead on the songs. As always, "C'est La Vie" got the best response, especially after it started receiving radio play.

"There's something about 'C'est La Vie,' especially because it's our first song," Keavy admitted later. "When you perform it, it just makes you go, 'Yeah!' no matter how many hundreds and thousands of times we've performed it."

There were a few who thought the lyrics of the song were full of double entendres, but, Sinead said, "It depends which way you look at them. When 'C'est La Vie' first came out there were a lot of people saying to us, 'Nudge, nudge, wink, wink—we know what you're really talking about this, that, and the other . . .' and to be honest, we hadn't even thought about that at all. It was completely innocent."

It wasn't just the band that thought so. From the day of its release, on May 25, 1998 (a day the girls will never forget) it was in heavy rotation on radio stations all over. The video saw plenty of action on MTV. It was perfect pop music, with a slight hip-hop beat, great harmonies, lots of little hooks—everything anyone could ask for in a pop song, in other words.

The record—and B*Witched themselves—was launched with a massive party. Epic took over The Talk of London club in Covent Garden for the event, flying in Sony representatives from all over the world, as well as masses of television, radio, and press people. The venue was decorated in orange and blue—which the girls had designated as the B*Witched colors—and there were B*Witched cookies and cakes on every table. The families of all the girls came over from Dublin—there was no way they were going to miss something like this! It was a proud moment for all the parents as the girls got up on the stage to perform. It was just a short set, with "C'est La Vie" as the highlight, of course. As they finished, fireworks went off around the stage, covering everything in glitter—another B*Witched trademark. For the rest of the evening, as everyone enjoyed themselves, the video of "C'est La Vie" kept playing. Now all they could do was wait, and see how the public reacted.

They'd hoped for the best, and truly believed it would do well, but nothing could have prepared them for the reaction the single got. On the very first week of its release, it went straight to the top of the charts—crashing in right at the Number One position! That wasn't unheard of, but for a band's debut it was pretty incredible.

They were still on tour with 911 when the news came out, and when the call came "we started crying, then laughing, and then went really quiet," Sinead recalled. "That evening we were on stage in Southampton and the D.J. announced to the people in the audience that we were Number One," Keavy continued. "We just went mad. It was brilliant 'cause the crowd enjoyed it as much of us!"

They'd come from nowhere and conquered the charts on their very first attempt. They felt on top of the world, as if this really *was* meant to be, and that maybe there was some special magic around them. Certainly some fairy godmother seemed to be smoothing the way for them.

But what were four girls with a hit single their first time out supposed to do? The answer, obviously, was party. Party, but not party hearty. Once the 911 tour was over, Epic took the lasses out to Planet Hollywood in London to celebrate their success in a big way. It wasn't merely that they'd justified the label's faith in them, it was that they were nice girls, too. Everyone was happy for them—it really couldn't have happened to four nicer people. The only one who didn't feel in the best mood was Edele. That morning she'd been to the dentist and had one of her wisdom teeth removed, so she was on medication and rather groggy. Still, there was no way she was going to miss this, even if she tended to sit quietly in her corner all night. They settled in at a big table, and the evening began.

"We had lots of big cakes and they gave us a swanky Sony video camera to film ourselves having fun for our Website. It was really great!" The people from Epic had gone to a lot of trouble to make it a fun-filled night, although some bits were more enjoyable than others.

"Actually, it was a bit embarrassing because they played our video on a massive screen," Lindsay recalled. "Everyone in the restaurant started singing along and we had to join in!" But for what the song had given them, and being in the spirit of things, they were singing louder than anyone else. Once 10:30 rolled around, however, the girls had to pack up and leave. The next day was full off commitments, and they wanted to be sure and get their sleep. As Keavy said, "It's a night we'll never forget, though." And how could they? Their very first Number One single, something every artist dreams about—something they'd all dreamed about before, and now it was a reality.

On the way home from Planet Hollywood, the girls discussed how they could celebrate the success among themselves, something they could do that would be just for them. And then one of them had a brilliant idea. Would it be a trip to a Caribbean island? A limo? No, in true pop star fashion, why not buy themselves a washing machine. The house hadn't come with one, and it meant they wouldn't have to keep hauling bags down to the Laundromat. And so, the next time they had a free day they went to an appliance store and picked one out—a heavy-duty one, possibly, to cope with the clothes of four girls, including a lot of denim. It was their present to themselves, and they felt particularly proud when it was set up in the kitchen. Unfortunately, they'd forgotten one thing. It was all well and good having a washer, but it really helped if you had a dryer, too, and they hadn't splashed out on that, which was going to cause a few problems.

"We still don't have a tumble dryer yet, though," Keavy admitted, "which is a shame because damp denim isn't very comfortable, you know!"

Still, all things considered, that was a minor complaint. They could afford one—if they could find the time to go and buy it. A top single made them into a very hot property, and suddenly everyone wanted to be bewitched. They'd been after the hit record, but they hadn't anticipated everything that came with it, even though Keavy and Edele had seen what happened with Shane in Boyzone. Everyone wanted a piece of them, and, perhaps not unnaturally, they found themselves saddled with a tag they'd rather not have had—the Irish Spice Girls.

It was probably inevitable. The meteoric rise of all things Spice had changed the face of popular music on the planet. Their records outsold everyone else's; there was simply no touching them. The Spice Girls were a phenomenon without precedent, and any other girl group coming along really had no chance of *not* being compared to them. It didn't matter if those comparisons were apt or not; they were simply bound to happen.

In the case of B*Witched, there was no similarity between the two bands. The Spice Girls would not have been seen dead in anything as ordinary as denim, and nor would they have taken to the stage wearing trainers (except for Sporty, of course). Not were they trained dancers—the main reason B*Witched always wear their trainers on stage is so they can move better and execute all those complex moves. So, in part, it was a difference of image. But it was more than that. In everything, B*Witched are more casual. Their music has a teenage sensibility that wasn't part of the Spices makeup at all. Perhaps the only point where they intersect is that Posh loves stuff from Prada, and one of the presents Epic gave B*Witched when "C'est La Vie" went to Number One was bags from Prada. Still, as Keavy said, "It's quite flattering in a way, because their success has been unbelievable. So to be compared to them is really cool."

Very quickly, though, they were beating those comparisons and being accepted for themselves, as four Irish girls with a lot of talent. Already, everything that was happening was way beyond their wildest dreams. The first time they sat down to watch themselves on *Top of the Pops*, Britain's leading television chart show, and something they'd all watched religiously, they had to pinch themselves to be sure it was real.

Every day was crammed. There were television appearances, photo shoots, more interviews—everybody wanted a piece of B*Witched. And there was still work to be done on their album, which was now due in the fall. For the girls, that was the main priority. They were still writing, and there was material they wanted to record. In fact, "Castles in the Air" was written "about how we felt when our Number One was 'C'est La Vie' in the U.K. We went straight into the studio and wrote that song. The inspiration was how we felt," explained Edele. So even success could bring great new songs.

By and large the album was complete by June. It had to be, with time to be allowed for cover design, manufacture, distribution, and all the other business elements that were a part of the complete package.

As the single finally receded down the charts, the girls had a chance to catch their breath. The next single wasn't due until September, and the album, which was simply going to be titled *B*Witched*, wasn't due until October. They could finally relax, and let reality catch up with them. That meant some time in Ireland, of course, but most of it was spent in Surrey, so they could be close to London when they were needed.

They'd quickly settled into a routine at the house. Where most boy bands could probably use a cleaner, a maid, *and* a cook, the girls were very self-sufficient. They all knew how to cook, and it was something they all did. Not much fast food for them—they all preferred home-cooked meals, something good and hearty. Being so active, they really didn't have to worry about what they ate, although they all tend to stay away from red meat. They even had a cleaning routine for the place, and followed it very carefully. While the dining room tended to become known as the "bag room"—where they left bags of stuff they'd bought or been given—the rest of the place was always spotless. And that was true even when they weren't home, it turned out.

"Once I'd left the dishes, and when we got back, they were washed!" Edele marveled. "I was like, 'Who did them?' Then a few things happened: Keavy's bed was made and her pajamas had been put away." At first the girls wondered if they had a ghost with a cleanliness fetish, but eventually they discovered the truth. The landlord's mother, who'd taken a real shine to the girls, and who knew just how busy they were, had come in a few times to help them out by tidying up!

The house was something of an oasis. Of course, some fans found out where they lived and camped out, waiting for autographs—which the girls happily gave them. Others would even knock on the door to meet them. For the most part, though, they weren't hounded by fans, certainly not in the way boy bands are. There was a real politeness to the B*Witched fans, something the band really appreciated. From Shane, Edele and Keavy had learned just how crazy some fans could be, but it wasn't something they experienced firsthand. So the house became a place they could relax, and wander around without makeup, just being themselves. One thing it wasn't was party central. The girls weren't big partygoers anyway, and the idea of hosting one simply didn't appeal to them at all. Besides, who would they invite? In England they only really knew people who were part of the music business. Their real friends were still back home in Ireland, and they couldn't all fly over for a Saturday night party, although one or two did come to visit.

Anyone who thought that all pop stars lived in luxury would have been shocked by the B*Witched house. It wasn't a mansion—not even close. It was a two-story, two-bedroom duplex in a fairly small town close to London. Nothing special, no massive garden. The girls lived very orderly, quiet lives. The stereo didn't blare loudly, disturbing the neighbors. In the evening, if they were home, the television would be on, catching the soaps and a movie. No late hours—their morning calls were usually too early to burn the candle at both ends, and the girls were true professionals; they knew that work came before a social life.

They actually liked the separation of public and private lives. Being quiet at home, there weren't always journalists and photographers on the doorstep. And because they hadn't had exciting pasts, like some of the Spice Girls, for example, they didn't have to face all kinds of embarrassing articles in the tabloids. They really were cleaner than clean—no old boyfriends able to drag up lurid tales or anything like that. Their biggest indulgence, really, was collecting teddy bears! They'd settled easily and well into living together away from home. For Sinead it was nothing new, of course, but the others had all been nervous about it. In the end, though, it worked perfectly. And it made sense for them to share a house. That way they were all together under one roof, so when they had to travel there was no collecting them from different apartments, or hoping someone hadn't overslept. Their biggest worry was Sinead forgetting something, which always seemed to happen! And since they always traveled together, and did everything together, being a band, it was simply easier for all of them.

Even after "C'est La Vie" had gone to Number One,

they still kept shopping in the local stores. Well, how could they not? Sure, they were recognized and asked for autographs, but it was all done in a very nice way, never pushy. None of them wanted to be isolated by fame. At heart they were all very normal, ordinary girls. The clothes they wore, onstage and off, all came from department stores, the same clothes any of their fans could buy. They wanted to live normal lives, and that meant being able to pop out for a pint of milk if they were running low. They had no need of all kinds of personal assistants, or anything like that. In fact they'd have felt downright uncomfortable having to deal with all of that. They even handled their own airline tickets, and still often used public transportation, like the bus, the train, and the Underground. No real star treatment for them!

Basically, the only thing sudden stardom gave them was a lot more work. But that was okay, really. This was what they'd wanted from their lives, and now they'd got it—in a much bigger way, and much sooner, than any of them could ever have imagined.

Of course, having debuted with a Number One single, that meant the expectations for a follow-up and for the album were extremely high, which put a lot of pressure on the girls. The last girl group to get a chart topper on their first single had been the Spice Girls, so everyone believed B*Witched could be just as big. Probably the only ones not putting pressure on them were the girls themselves. Sure, they wanted everything they released to do well, but mostly they wanted it to sound good. That was success to them; if it sold incredibly well, that was a major bonus.

This was the time of their lives. Their dreams had all come true, so quickly and so fully. It really was like magic, and somehow they believed they couldn't have picked a more apt name. Britain had fallen under their spell too (and so had Ireland, but that was almost a foregone conclusion, given their background), but there was still a wide world out there to be conquered. And, of course, plans were afoot for that. If the U.K. adored them, why not everywhere else, too?

One major hit single could have been pure luck, a case of the right song at the right time. There were plenty of one-hit wonders in the history of music. What the girls needed was another big record to prove there was more to them. But the record company was in no hurry. As "C'est La Vie" slipped down the charts, no follow-up was rushed out to capitalize on its success. There was plenty of time for that. Epic believed in the girls as much as they believed in themselves. The next single wouldn't come out until the fall, to act as a trailer and a teaser for the album, which would be released in October.

That didn't mean no one was working on the band's behalf, or that the band was able to take the entire summer off. It had already been decided that the new single would be "Rollercoaster," the song the girls had written about the way their life had become (and not about a roller coaster ride). It made a good choice, an upbeat follow-up. The one irony was that, really, Edele hated roller coasters, and would never go on one. But when it came time to shoot the video, she might have been willing to go on one rather than spend hour upon hour suspended in a harness. Actually, she got into the idea fairly quickly, although she was exhausted when it was over.

"We were nervous about the harnesses we had to wear at first," she recalled. "But it didn't take us long to get used to them. We were soon tumbling around having fun! And we really do look like we can fly!"

It was probably the toughest challenge the girls had faced, tougher even than that first appearance on Irish television or that first night opening for Boyzone. It was a seventeen-hour shoot for the video, and the girls spent most of that tucked into fairly uncomfortable harnesses, having to look as if they were totally enjoying themselves. They were supposed to be flying—and in the finished video clip, that was exactly what it would seem as if they were doing—and having fun. But after seventeen hours of doing one thing, it stops being fun. Of course, they were just suspended and moved around a little. The flying was added by special effect later, and very convincing it was, too. But there was no way any of the girls could ever forget the video shoot.

A lot was riding on "Rollercoaster." If it hit, then it proved the girls' previous Number One was more than a fluke. And it would bode well for the release of the album. If it bombed, then the album would still appear, but the lasses might as well have thought about moving back to Dublin and working retail again. In other words, it was exactly the kind of pressure everyone needs!

So there was plenty of tension and excitement in the B*Witched household on September 25, 1998. What they all wanted, more than anything, was to be able to continue with this, to keep their dream a reality. But it was out of their hands. It was all going to be decided by D.J.s playing the record, and by the public buying it—or not.

The single, backed by a track that wouldn't appear on the album, "Get Happy" (a song which was also on the American release of "C'est La Vie), appeared in mid-September. The cover picture of the girls in a boxing ring, all wearing red boxing gloves, was cute, but not totally inspirational. This was going to be sold on the strength of the music, not anything else.

While the girls held their breath to see how it was received, the record raced out of the stores almost as quickly as "C'est La Vie." B*Witched hadn't just enchanted their record company, they'd also put a spell on the British public, too. Now it was selling, the other big question was—could it do as well as the last one? They'd set a standard the last time out; now, if the single didn't go all the way to the top, people could say they were "slipping." That would be far from true, of course, but there were always those who looked for any excuse to put people down.

The band had no need to worry. They managed to do it

all a second time around. Yes, "Rollercoaster" followed its predecessor all the way to Number One—the most amazing feeling any of the band had ever had. To do it once was extraordinary, but to have your first *two* releases both go to Number One—how did you get your head around that?

By screaming a lot and crying—all for joy, of course. That was all they could do. They'd had high hopes, but this went way beyond them. It was like having everything you'd ever dreamed of put in your lap.

The release of *B*Witched* was less than a month away. But before that happened, the girls were going to be doing a lot of traveling as Sony (Epic's parent company) began releasing "C'est La Vie" all over Europe. Just as it had in Britain, it proved irresistible. Germany, Holland, Belgium, France, Italy, and Sweden were captivated by it—and that meant the girls were all over the Continent, promoting it. If it felt weird to be pushing this song again when they had a new Number One where they lived, they didn't show it. But even when they were abroad, their thoughts still centered on business at home. To be honest, their rapid success still stunned them a little.

"We're still a bit shaky," Keavy said in Sweden. " 'C'est La Vie' was the big hit of the summer. And then we got an autumn hit, too. Now we are a bit nervous about the album and the next single. But we hope for the best. Now it feels good that we have fans that will support us."

The fans had supported the singles. But would they spend a lot more money on an album by *B*Witched*? Everyone hoped so. With "Rollercoaster" still close to the top of the charts, the album came out in October—and entered that chart at Number Three. It wasn't Number One (and nor would it climb that high, thwarted in part by a George Michael *Best Of* that appeared shortly after), but that didn't matter; it was still a huge success. The girls did something they'd normally never do—they threw a party.

Not at home in Surrey, of course. They booked a London restaurant, The Collection, for a Sunday lunchtime (remember, no late nights for these girls) and invited all their friends. A few were able to come over from Ireland, a few traveled in from Surrey. A lot were part of the music business, like the guys from 911, the band B*Witched had opened for on their first British tour. Boyzone weren't in the country, so Shane couldn't share in his sisters' happiness. But he was there in spirit, just as all the families were. It wasn't a bigger moment than the two Number One singles, but it was every bit as gratifying. Now no one could ever say that B*Witched hadn't made it!

If there was one theme that ran through the entire record, it was the Irishness of the sound. Sometimes it was very obvious, as on the opener, "Let's Go (The B*Witched Jig)," while at other times it was just a sensibility. But it served to unify the very different sounds on the songs on the album.

"Our songs are very positive and happy," Edele explained. "All of us like a wide variety of music, so it's not all one style. We have pop music, a little rock, a little drum and bass—but the Irish music runs through all of it." If fact, Edele pointed out, it would have been impossible to make the album as it stood without the fiddle running all the way through it.

It opened with "Let's Go (The B*Witched Jig)" whose first thirty seconds were hauntingly Irish and romantic, evocative of all those Irish ballads, before Edele shouted in the fiddle, the beats kicked in, and the fiddle began playing at hyperspeed, a jig gone completely mad, the highest energy you could imagine to put listeners into the perfect frame of mind for the rest of the record. This was Irish music even for those who hated Irish music, propelled by the club rhythms into something new and rather different. It was both an introduction to the record, and something of a manifesto, a way of saying "We're Irish and we're proud of it, but we're also a new generation."

Just how much of a new generation became obvious in the next track, the truly magical "C'est La Vie." With more hooks than a fishing boat, it was probably one of the best singles released in the Nineties, a piece of perfect pop music. Even the backing vocals, with their "oh-oh's," made for another hook. There was some scratching behind it all, a pretty simple tune, some clever catchy lyrics, and a perfect singalong quality about it all, leading into the irresistible chorus. Edele kept the Irishness alive in her little asides. But where it all took off was in the middle instrumental section, which could have come out of a hip version of *Riverdance*, the fiddle and whistle playing a jig together (and the girls might have done more for step dancing among a younger crowd than all the productions of *Riverdance* put together). There was also a fresh, schoolyard quality about the whole thing—it could easily make a great skipping rhyme.

"Rev It Up" was completely different, although that was the idea, of course. No two songs were going to sound alike, or even belong to the same school of music, other than they were all pop and all had an Irish flavor. "Rev It Up" was an ideal summer tune, the type of thing to play with the top down, driving around in the sunshine—and that was what it was about, in a sense, enjoying yourself, gunning the motor and letting it go. It was a bit Seventies, opening with a sound similar to some early Jackson Five, back in the days when Michael was still a member. It was a little funky, and showed just how well the girls' voices worked together. The beats, though, were strictly Nineties, pushing it along while the girls sang of beaches and sunshine, something that made you think more of California than Galway! Then the fiddle tripped in and made the whole thing into a party—it really did add a certain something to the song, and set it apart. The song also showed all the critics who'd written them off as an Irish Spice girls that they were wrong. They were every bit as much fun, but they certainly weren't clones. They used their voices in different ways, and while they didn't trade lead vocal lines like the Spices, there was more going on in the background.

"To You I Belong" was a song with special meaning for Edele, Keavy, Sinead, and Lindsay; they'd written it for their mothers and fathers, who'd all supported them totally in pursuing a singing career—in everything they did, in fact. The sentiments were very real and very honest. Again, it was a change of pace, slowing it all down to a ballad, but after a high-energy start, that was necessary. It was one of nine songs the girls had co-written on the album, quite a high number, and they had every reason to be proud of their efforts. Then again, they'd put months of work into all this—these weren't knockoffs, by any means. They'd been rehearsed, polished, and perfected over a long period. The song began with sweeping keyboard chords and a guitar line before Edele began singing. Over her voice there was a whistle line, keeping that Irish flavor in the background. The fiddle was there, too, doubling up with the whistle between verses. Lyrically, it could have either been for their parents (which it was) or to some unnamed boyfriend, a lovely romantic ballad.

The tempo moved back up to mid-pace on "Rollercoaster,' similar to from both the Seventies (echoes of Fleetwood Mac's "Don't Stop") and the Sixties (shades of the Beatles' psychedelic period on the bridge), carefully melded together over some hip-hop beats to create a confection as tasty as fresh cotton candy—and every bit as sweet. It had been B*Witched's second Number One, of course, and it was easy to see why—it was simply great pop music. A bit more restrained that "C'est La Vie," but with a killer chorus. Written about their own experiences, the way things had taken off for them, it was joyful, very open, and again it really showcased those fabulous harmonies, keeping the fiddle in the middle section. Not playing an Irish line this time, but it was hardly necessary; even without that, it reminded you that this was an Irish band, as if anyone could ever forget!

"Blame It on the Weatherman" was another ballad, and one of the best on the album. It was also one of only two tracks to feature strings. The arrangement was clever, with plucked strings simulating the sound of falling rain. Really, it was one of the best post-breakup songs of the decade, stirring and romantic, but still remarkably catchy, and with its chorus made from the title, a phrase truly taken from everyday life. It also showed just what a strong voice Edele possessed, and how effectively and emotionally she could use it. Not that the others were slouches, either, using their voices to color Edele's words, and glide in behind her to fill the spaces beautifully. There was a tremendously natural feel to the way they all sang together; their voices just seemed to fit. It really was magic when they all opened their mouths in unison.

Lyrically, there wasn't a whole lot to "We Four Girls," but that didn't matter too much. It was meant to be something of a dance track, but with its strong guitar work, there was a definite alternative rock (known as "indie" in Britain) side to the whole thing. It would work both in a club and on the radio. Definitely heavier and less poppy than the rest of the record, it came at you like a curve ball, but that was good. There was no law saying the band had to be all about one thing, and they weren't going to be.

"We don't really think about limits," said Keavy, and this proved it, as artistically credible as any of the Brit pop bands around, and showing the girls to be totally versatile. Moving from something very dance-y during the verses to some crunching guitar work during the chorus, it got in your face and forced you to pay attention. These four girls weren't going anywhere; they were sticking around for a long time. Perhaps the best thing was that they felt adventurous and confident enough to include a track like this, that broke the mold and stood outside the standard pop guidelines.

From there it was a big jump to the balladry of "Castles in the Air." This was the song the girls had written after

"C'est La Vie" hit the top spot as a single. Over a percolating synthesizer line, playing some R&B changes, came a song that could easily have been sung by someone like Mariah Carey—although this came without the vocal gymnastics. There was a very spare beauty to the arrangement, with the backing vocals like a cushion under the lead. Again, it was one of those things that could easily be misinterpreted, if you didn't know the real story. But that was the point—you could take it however you wanted. And when the four girls went into the smooth "ooohs" after the break, it could almost give you goosebumps from its loveliness.

"Freak Out" took a completely different tack. Its opening was similar to a 1970 hit, "Venus," by a Dutch band, Shocking Blue, one that came out long before the girls were born. But that had been a great song, and so was this. Once the vocals entered, though, there was no mistaking this for anyone but B*Witched. Over some dance beats, there was some hip-hop rapping that took the listener by surprise before exploding into the chorus that invited you to sing and dance along. It was probably one of the best mixes of rock, hip-hop, and dance that had been put together, mainly because it was so seamless, and the "party" sounds in the background suited it perfectly.

Another ballad, "Like the Rose," was introduced by a very Irish line, the whistle playing over the keyboards. At first it seemed like it was just going to be a vocal workout for Edele, then the others joined in on the chorus. The changes, and even the rose image, were quite Celtic, making sure that stayed a part of the music. In some ways, with the chord changes, it was the most sophisticated song on the album.

"Never Giving Up" took the beats per minute quite a bit higher, with a hip-hop beat, strong guitars on the intro that led into a pure pop song, and Edele's vocals supported by a bouncy keyboard line that led into a powerful chorus about love. Quite trickily, the arrangement mixed guitar and keyboards for a sound that walked a very fine line between rock and pop. The chorus just stuck in your brain, and when it came in after the song's middle section, it seemed to simply explode out of the speakers, before dissolving like sparkles from a skyrocket, only to return again a new key—a brilliant piece of arranging.

Then came the last track, "Oh, Mr. Postman." This would have the girls signing off with a big orchestral ballad. There was a very Sixties pop feel to it, particularly in the backing vocals, that owed a lot of the Beatles. Once again, this track was very different from anything else on the album, heavily arranged, to the point where it could easily have gone over the top. But it didn't. It stayed on this side of good taste, being emotional rather than bombastic. There was even a cheeky little tribute to Seventies band ELO right at the end, with a voice put through a vocoder. And then it was over.

The Tours

*I*T WAS AN ABSOLUTE TRIumph of a record. Not just for the fact that it entered the chart at Number Three (and though it didn't go any higher, that was achievement enough) and sold plenty of copies. Artistically it was a total success. To be fair, it was short, clocking in at a little under forty minutes. But the quality was there on every track. The girls themselves had co-written nine of the twelve songs, along with Ray Hedges, and really put them on the line. A lot of the responsibility was theirs, they'd been willing to take risks, and it had paid off.

A lot of credit, too, went to Hedges, who excelled himself on the album, both as producer and arranger. "We've got a really good team," Sinead pointed out. "I don't think anybody is 'in control.' Record company or producer or artists, it's everybody working together."

And teamwork really was the secret. Everyone had worked as hard as they could to make B*Witched successful, commercially *and* artistically. They could have taken the easy route and brought in songs, then just sung them, but that wouldn't have been satisfying. Instead the girls had poured their hearts and souls into the idea, probably more than anyone else. After all, in the final instance it would be them up on the stage singing the words, and they wanted it all to be convincing and real.

Musically, few bands, and specifically pop bands, had covered as many bases on one record. It could easily have seemed like a big tangle, moving from one thing to the next, but that Irish sound gave it a real thread, a continuity. And each song was so strong that it all managed to work, even though on paper it shouldn't. It was the kind of album labels dream about, that truly did have something for everyone.

And that was why even more markets were interested in releasing it. Having seen the phenomenal success in Britain, and then in Europe, there was interest from all over the globe. And that meant a bit of traveling for the girls—who no longer trusted forgetful Sinead with their airline tickets.

First up was a trip to the other side of the world, starting in Japan, and then moving on to Australia. They all loved traveling, and now they were getting to do it. And, since they were now officially stars, it was all in style—first-class all the way. Tokyo turned out to be very cool, not a bit the way they'd expected it, neither quaintly Asian nor a science-fiction city, but just a normal, big place, not unlike London. The same was true for Sydney, except they spoke English there, and had a long, deep love of all things Irish.

In both places it was a case of meeting with record executives, then putting on showcase performances for the suits and the media, a chance for them to get out and strut their stuff, which they hadn't had a chance to do lately.

With missions accomplished, and everybody won over (how could they not be, after the exuberance of a B*Witched performance?), it was time to complete their round-the-world trip, by hitting America—specifically New York.

While Edele and Keavy had been there before as part of the Dublin Allstars, it was new to Lindsay and Sinead. And a completely magical place. Loud, always on the go, but it had a kind of energy that kept them going through their jet lag. Their main reason for being in the city was to talk to the people at Epic in the U.S. about releasing the album, and to perform yet another showcase for media people. This time, though, there would be a twist to the proceedings. The showcase would be held at an Irish pub called Connolly's.

Of course it was a success, and Epic was quickly plotting a strategy for the girls in America. Amazingly, though, they weren't going to rush "C'est La Vie" out before Christmas. They'd wait until well in the New Year, and let the lasses have some exposure first doing what they did best—singing live in front of people.

With all that wrapped up, and foreign deals in the bag, it was time to go home again. But that didn't mean Ireland. It was back to Surrey, and back to work. They'd had two Number Ones in Britain—could they make it three? And more importantly, could they have a Christmas Number One? Maybe in the long run being at the top on that particular week wasn't such a big deal, but it was seen that way. Seasonal songs always did well over the holidays, and so did ballads. Since the band wasn't about to pop back into the studio to record a Christmas song, it was decided instead to release one of the ballads off *B*Witched*, "To You I Belong."

The girls couldn't have been happier. Since they'd written it for their parents, it had a lot of resonance for them. It would be backed with a couple of songs that hadn't seen the light of day before, "Fly Away," and "B*Witched's Message to Santa," a funny little seasonal throwaway.

A new single meant a new video. And in this case, it also meant new outfits. There was still a lot of denim, of course, but decidedly more upscale than they'd been before, a move away from the High Street stores and into designer territory.

The video itself looked as if it had been filmed in a gorgeous ice cavern, but that was just special effects trickery. The shoot took place in a bare studio, using what is called "blue screen" photography. In other words, the girls performed in front of a blue backdrop, and then their images were superimposed on another backdrop—in this case the ice cavern. It was very well done, enough to fool the casual viewer.

"To You I Belong" was a known quantity, of course, but "Fly Away" certainly wasn't. It was quite different for the band—something that almost become a trademark of theirs. It was another ballad, soft and smooth, with lots of acoustic guitar, almost Brazilian and jazzy in its feel. Maybe it wasn't as strong as most of the tracks on the album—probably one reason it hadn't appeared before—but it was still very lovely, Edele hitting the high notes, and the others contributing some cloud-like backing vocals.

"B*Witched's Message to Santa" was pure goof, a fake phone message to Santa Claus that doubled as a message to their fans. Running less than a minute, it was sweet, pure Irish, and a lot of fun.

With their track record so far, and an early December release date for the single, the odds looked quite good that the girls could make it three in a row *and* have that coveted Christmas Number One. But they were going to be facing some very serious competition, in the form of the Spice Girls.

The Spices had done a massive concert in London in September, finishing off their world tour there. There'd been plenty of turmoil in their camp, with Geri having left, and the remainder carrying on as a quartet. Their new single, "Goodbye," supposedly about Geri leaving, would be their first record as a four-piece, and it was set to come out just in time for Christmas. So it was going to be a face-off of the girl groups, which made for a lot of good press.

The Spice girls had seen their first three singles go to Number One. If "To You I Belong" managed to hit the top, B*Witched would have equaled that feat. It would have made them, beyond any shadow of a doubt, one of Britain's biggest bands. So there was a lot riding on this, apart from any supposed rivalry (which didn't exist) between them and the Spices.

Neither Lindsay, Edele, Sinead, nor Keavy knew what to expect. Just because they'd had two Number Ones didn't mean that the third would automatically follow. It would have been too much to hope for, getting a hat-trick like that. And even more to have a Christmas Number One.

But the record totally surprised them—it entered the chart right at the top on its first week. Three in a row. It was official; they were huge. But could they hang on for a second week, that magical week over Christmas?

That turned out to be one feat they couldn't manage. The lure of a new Spice Girls single, released the week after theirs, was simply too strong. It didn't matter, however. They'd done something they'd never have believed possible during those first days at Digges Lane.

They still got to appear on the special Christmas edition of *Top of the Pops*, which rounded up the year's Number One hits. And they also had a good laugh doing it. Keavy and Edele decided to play a practical joke, changing their hair and clothes (Keavy put red extensions in her hair), and appearing as each other. Everyone in the audience was fooled (except perhaps their parents, who saw it all on television)—even Lindsay and Sinead couldn't recognize the difference!

It was a great way to round out what had been a magnificent year. Three top singles, performances all over the globe, lots of television. They'd even met royalty, when they appeared on the *Royal Variety Show*, doing a medley of their songs, and ended up shaking hands with Prince Charles (not a noted fan of pop music). What more could four Irish girls ask for out of a twelve-month period?

A bit of a break was the answer, and they got it right after Christmas. Sinead, Keavy, and Edele went back to Ireland for a short holiday, while Lindsay flew to Athens to spend a little time with her parents.

They were going to need all the rest they could get, though. It looked like 1999 was going to start with a big bang for them all. They'd seen New York already. Now they were going to see a lot more of America as they undertook their first tour there. And not just any tour. They were going to be one of the opening acts for 'N Sync, the boy band who'd just gone mega after their own success everywhere on the planet. That was going to be a major challenge. With no record out in the U.S., and "C'est La Vie" not even due in stores until February, they'd be playing to audiences that knew nothing about them. More than that, audiences who wanted only to see the five boys they loved. It wasn't going to be easy.

The girls weren't about to let something like that faze them. They were ready, rehearsed, and up to anything life could throw at them. America was going to mean starting all over again, but they weren't proud—they didn't mind doing that. If anything, it would bring out the very best in them, and make them sing and dance better than ever.

They'd seen New York, but if they thought the rest of America was going to be like that, they were in for a shock. Their first surprise was at just how huge the country was; it took as long to fly from New York to the West Coast as it did to fly from New York to Ireland.

And, as Edele noted, "When we first came to the U.S., we weren't sure what to expect from the audience—nobody had really heard of us, and people were coming to see one of the biggest boy bands in the country." They'd been told not to expect a huge reaction, but they were very pleasantly surprised at what happened. Right from the beginning, the crowds got into what they were doing, and would start waving their arms and dancing to the songs. That made for an encouraging start.

While their short time on stage was gratifying, for the most part the girls had to endure a lot of traveling and boredom. It wasn't unusual for them to be on a bus for ten hours between cities. And while they got to see the real America, it wasn't quite what they'd have chosen for themselves.

'N Sync proved to be very gracious hosts to the girls,

but they were in such demand that there was very little chance to socialize. They did get to spend a little time with Joey, the most gregarious of the bunch, but that was about it. They boys were so busy, they didn't even have time to attend their own after-show party, leaving B*Witched just sitting there, not knowing a soul around!

Although they were well-received, for the first part of the tour audiences were still wondering "Who are they?" about these four girls. They didn't have a record out, no one had heard of them; they were a total mystery (the same was true of the other opening act, Britney Spears—obviously it was a lucky tour to be on!). Once "C'est La Vie" appeared in stores in February, however, things quickly changed. "Within the last week, we could see that growing with the audience," Edele said.

Just as it had everywhere else, the song had hit written all over it in America. As well as a strong song on its own merits, it also served as a teaser for the upcoming album, with snippets of "We Four Girls," "Rollercoaster," and "To You I Belong." There was the hilarious "B*Witched Quiz Show," a spoken word track that was a take off of ... quiz shows, starring who else but Keavy, Edele, Sinead, and Lindsay. Finally there was a non-album cut, "Get Happy," which had previously appeared in Britain with the "Rollercoaster" single. Again co-written by the band, the chord sequence wasn't a million miles from "C'est La Vie," although the feel was very different, with a strong emphasis on the beat. It was much rockier, with lots of guitar work, finding a place somewhere between rock and funk once it hit a groove. Again, it was easy to see why this hadn't ended up on the album. It was good, but not in the same class as the tunes that had made the final cut; it simply lacked that special sparkle. Still, it served notice to America that the girls were very much about more than one thing.

Of course, America succumbed to "C'est La Vie." It was a song that appealed right across the board, to all ages, and within three weeks of its release, it was comfortably nestled in the Top Twenty. The biggest surprise was that it didn't hit the top spot, although there was plenty of competition out there, not the least from their concert colleague, Britney herself.

Not that the girls were too disappointed. America had always been considered the hardest nut to crack, and if they hadn't opened it all the way, they'd still made a very strong impact the first time out.

There was more to zigzagging around America than just playing 'N Sync concerts (as if that wasn't quite enough). They'd also agreed to do a mini-tour of some malls around the country, all sponsored by Hello Kitty cosmetics, with whom the band had signed a contract. By the late Nineties this kind of thing had become quite common, after being pioneered by Tiffany, another teen artist, a decade before. Back then, a lot of people had regarded it as a joke. Now it made sense, taking the music to the place where the kids hung out. Mall shows drew great crowds, often in the thousands, and was a fantastic way of breaking bands in, letting people get to hear them and meet them.

For B*Witched, that meant a total of seven malls, and a quick introduction to mall culture, something that didn't exist in Britain or Ireland (they had shopping malls, but they weren't teen hangouts; over there, no one knew what a mallrat was). And it meant they were performing for their own audience, people who'd come to see *them*, not 'N Sync. It made for a much more crowded schedule, not to mention a lot more driving, but those were sacrifices they were all prepared to make.

"We did just the set we normally do, except 'We Four Girls,' and then afterward we did a signing for about an hour and a half... the kids loved it."

They most certainly did. At each mall appearance, the girls were bringing in average crowds of three thousand, huge for a band that was still basically unknown. And each time they were getting a massive reaction—you're not signing autographs for an hour and a half if no one wants to see you!

While some of it seemed so familiar to them, Lindsay, Sinead, Keavy, and Edele did find a lot of America to be a culture shock. The television, more than anything, was a surprise. They were already familiar with shows like *South Park* and *Friends*. Now they had a chance to get into the daytime fare. No, not more soap operas, but the talk shows like *Jerry Springer* and *Change of Heart*. They quickly found themselves hooked on both (which might have meant they were far more American at heart than they thought). Probably more than anything, though, it was the sheer size of America that overwhelmed them. At home they were used to people walking places; in America, at least the way they saw it, people drove everywhere. The parking lots were jammed, the stores were crowded, but there was no one on the street! To them it was all quite bizarre, but by the time they'd been in the U.S. for six weeks, they'd acclimated to it all.

All in all, their time in America was a great success. They'd made a lot of friends, and their shows had brought them a lot of fans, as well as serving to promote the single, which had done stirring business in terms of sales—it would eventually go gold, with more than half a million copies sold. And it primed everyone for the release of the album in April, which would be their next big American test.

They'd never spent this long on the road before. While they'd enjoyed the experience, there was no doubt they were exhausted by the time it was all over, ready to head home and give themselves a few days off to recover. Every night they'd given their all and won people over. Now it was time to chill a little—and that meant very little—before the hard work resumed.

There was a *lot* of hard work waiting for them at home. While it seemed as if their album had only just appeared, it was already time to start thinking of the next one, to begin writing and recording some basic tracks for Ray Hedges to work with. That was going to mean long, long hours in the studio.

And that wasn't all. There was a new single to be considered, and this would be the big one. If it went to Number One, they'd be the first girl group in the history of the U.K. charts to have their first four singles all reach the pole position—which would put them in the record books.

Almost any track could have been pulled from the album for a single. After a lot of thought, the record company chose Lindsay's favorite, "Blame It on the Weatherman," another ballad. Having had a summer hit, a fall hit, and a winter hit, now it was time to cover all the seasons and have a spring hit—at least that was what everyone hoped!

A new single also meant a new video, and no expense was going to be spared on this one. It also seemed to mean a change of image. Up until now, all four of the lasses had seemed very much like the girls next door, someone you could comfortably chat with on the street. They looked quite at home in their denims. The video stylist, however, had very different ideas this time around. The denim was still there—it just wouldn't have been B*Witched without it, but there was also a lot of leather, crop tops, and something much wilder, as if B*Witched had wandered onto the set of *Mad Max*. And to top it all off, quite literally, all four of them got new hairstyles. Lindsay's trademark curls were gone, and her hair was shaped into a short modified bob. Keavy went the freaky route, all gelled and spiky. Sinead now sported shorter hair, but still blond. Only Edele looked pretty much the same, but even she was wearing longer extensions. All of a sudden, these girls didn't look as if they'd just traveled across from Dublin or just walked out of the store with a new pair of jeans!

Maybe it was time for something different, or maybe not. But sometimes a change can make you feel good, and there was no denying that they all looked great, even as the threatening skies on the video loomed behind them.

"Blame It on the Weatherman" had been one of the album's big ballads, anyway. For the single, it was teamed with another ballad, "Together We'll Be Fine," about the difficulties of making a relationship work. It was relatively sparsely arranged, mostly just piano behind Edele's voice, and it was much more adult than most things they'd recorded before. Was that another sign for the future? It was hard to tell, really. Time would tell. The single's third track was an orchestral version of "Blame It on the Weatherman," which was exactly what it said—the girls backed by a full orchestra. It worked better than anyone might have expected, but it was the kind of song that suited such a full arrangement, although it was a little strange not to hear drums keeping time behind it all (at least on the first verse). It threw the voices into much greater relief, and made you realize, yet again, how well they worked together. In many ways, it was an elaborate remix. But however you thought of it, it worked beautifully.

The single's release, in March, 1999, had everyone full of expectations. There were even bets being made as to whether B*Witched could make it four in a row. Even the girls found themselves caught up in the excitement, as much as they could be, with so much going on. All their time was being spent in the studio, working on new material. The fact they hadn't allowed themselves to be limited to one (or even two or three) styles was going to work in their favor. It meant that on the new album they could do anything they wanted. They'd grown a lot since the first record, even though it was fairly recent, and they'd experienced a very great deal indeed. All of that would end up being reflected on the next record, in one way or another.

Meanwhile, the time between the single appearing and the charts being released seemed to last forever, although it was really just a matter of days. But as soon as the news appeared, there was celebration at Epic, and much more stunned joy in the B*Witched house. They'd done it! Four times in a row they'd released singles, and all four times they'd gone to Number One. The Spice Girls might have the big name recognition still, but it was B*Witched who'd broken the record. It truly was unbelievable, especially when you considered that just two years earlier, they were still all in Dublin. Things had moved incredibly fast.

When they appeared in public, they all looked happy, but shocked. And something else was quite noticeable— many of the changes that had been made for the video of "Blame It on the Weatherman" had gone; they'd simply been there for the shoot. They were back to being the lovable girls-next-door. That came as a relief to a lot of people, not least the girls themselves. Looking that way for a few hours was fine, but it took way too much work to maintain. At heart they were still a bunch of tomboys who all preferred as little makeup and primping as possible.

The writing for the album continued. Unlike the first time, though, they were on a tight deadline now, and that meant working every hour they could find. In a couple more weeks they'd be jetting away again, heading back to America for another long, grueling tour. Before they set foot on the plane they had to have everything ready, so when they returned they could go into the studio and really begin work on the finished product, which had already been penciled in for a fall release in Britain.

The trip to America was going to serve a double purpose. "C'est La Vie" was still on the charts, but it was almost time for the U.S. release of *B*Witched*. And what better way to promote it than to tour, which would also help consolidate the fan base they'd established the first time around. As if that wasn't *quite* enough, the whole thing would start off with the taping of a Disney Channel *In Concert*, which would mean the girls would have a few days in Los Angeles to enjoy the weather before they hit the road properly. Were they ready? Of course they were! They were all stoked at the prospect of being able to perform again, and they knew how to pace themselves for America now.

Last time out, they'd opened for one of the big two boy bands. This time around, they had the opening slot for one of the hottest new acts, 98°. The boys from Cincinnati were tearing it up all over the country (in May they'd take part in the biggest radio promotion in American history, in Buffalo, New York), and a ticket to see them was like gold. It made for a dynamic double bill. By now people really knew who B*Witched were, and they wanted to see them, too, not just the headliners. They all thought it would be brilliant.

The States

ONE THING THE GIRLS weren't afraid of was hard work, which was just as well, because they were going to see a lot of it between the start of April and the end of August. There would be not one, but two, exhausting tours of America, literally going coast to coast both times, and somehow, in between, they would have a few days in which to finish off their album. Probably more than anything they'd done in the past, this would be the real test for them. If they could happily survive the summer of '99, they could do anything.

Of course, a few days in Los Angeles at the end of March came as a very pleasant little break. It was warm and sunny, a big change from damp, chilly Surrey. Apart from their concert taping at Disneyland, they were free to roam the city, play a bit—and shop. That meant hitting some of the fancy stores on Rodeo Drive in Beverly Hills, and walking away with a few things (very few; the girls couldn't believe the prices). The play part came at Disneyland, just down the road in Anaheim, California. There they could be little girls again, having great fun on the rides, seeing the sights, having their pictures taken with Mickey, eating cotton candy, just totally indulging themselves.

Showtime was a different matter—for that they would be completely professional. They were sharing the bill, both on the stage and on the television *In Concert* program, with

5ive, the fab fivesome from England. The two bands already knew each other, of course. 5ive had hit it big in Europe, and had broken in the States with a single, just as B*Witched had. Now both were really trying to make themselves known.

Judging by the crowd around the stage, it seemed as if a lot of people were already familiar with them. The girls pulled out all the stops to entertain, nonstop singing and dancing, with Edele leading the way. During "C'est La Vie" they even had a fake fiddler join them for the Irish dancing, while their band played at the back of the stage. They were, of course, dressed in their trademark denim.

What aired on the Disney Channel was very much an abbreviated version of the full show. Each band only received half an hour, and some of that was taken up with interview footage. But it was enough to give a very strong idea what Sinead, Keavy, Lindsay, and Edele could do. And it was an important show to play. These *In Concert* specials had helped a lot of bands become huge, including 98°, Brandy, and 'N Sync. They were appointment viewing for a lot of teens and pre-teens. To play one meant you'd either arrived, or you were on the verge of being there.

It also made a good warm-up date for the tour, a chance to have fun doing a show, without all the pressure of traveling day in and day out. They sang, went back to their hotel rooms and simply chilled for a couple of days. But taking their rest when they could was probably a good idea; it was a commodity that was going to be in very short supply for a while. Over the next five-and-a-half weeks, the girls would be playing a total of twenty-nine dates. That didn't allow for much downtime. It was tight scheduling, but they knew they could do it. The 'N Sync tour hadn't been quite as grueling as this, but it let them know what to expect. Now, at least, they were prepared.

To say twenty-nine dates in thirty-six days sounded harsh enough, but when you considered that a number of those "free" days consisted of spending hours on a bus, traveling the freeways between cities, it just became totally excruciating. By the time it was over, they would be utterly fried. Even though they knew all that going in, it wasn't going to prevent them from giving their utmost at every single show. Not only did the fans deserve it, but their professional pride demanded it.

As the tour began, *B*Witched* had just been released in the U.S., and was already storming up the charts. It would hit Number Twelve—not as high as it had managed in other parts of the world, but still very far from shabby—and in just five weeks, it would go platinum, with over a million copies sold. That meant they'd hit that particular mark faster than the Spice Girls in the States, and, much more telling, quicker than any of the boy bands with their debuts. That was a real achievement. It automatically shot them into the major leagues as artists, and made this tour particularly important.

But much of 1999 would be spent concentrating on America. It was the biggest music market in the world, and hitting it big there meant you were a real power. This would be their second tour, and there was already a third being planned.

Oddly enough, for all their hits and records sold, B*Witched had yet to headline a tour anywhere. Even in Britain they'd only opened for other acts. One of their dreams, according to Edele, was to have their own, real tour, and that was already planned and confirmed for November, when they'd play a total of eight dates in Britain, all at massive arenas. It would start on the eighteenth in Newcastle, followed by Birmingham, Manchester, Brighton, Cardiff, Sheffield, Glasgow, and finishing up in Wembley, London, the place where the Spice Girls had completed their world tour some fourteen months before.

If it seemed as if B*Witched were being far more cautious than the Spices, that was definitely the case. Rather than plunging in, they were taking it little step by little step, building their audiences gradually. It was quite deliberate.

Move too fast, and they could easily end up falling on their faces, which no one wanted. This way they could not only build success, but make it last a very long time. The Spices were taking 1999 off, as Victoria and Mel B. became mothers. Who even knew if anyone would care when they decided to return. B*Witched would be there, carrying on, playing shows, releasing records. They didn't need to try and splash their names all over the papers for being outrageous. First of all, it would have gone against their natural personalities, and secondly, they were singers, not tabloid fodder. This was the way that worked for them. A little slower route to the top, but one that made them all happier.

The 98° tour kicked off just up the coast from Anaheim, in Berkeley, California, on April 2, before moving on to Sacramento on the third. It was an easy start, the two cities relatively close, with not much traveling. But then it would kick into a higher gear, and they'd really begin to feel it. In rapid succession there was Phoenix, Las Vegas, San Jose, and two dates in Los Angeles, before there was any kind of a break, and that was spent heading north to Salt Lake City. Even though they'd barely been off it, the girls were thrilled to be back on the road in America, and the shows just jammed.

"The tour has a lot of energy, and so do the crowds," Sinead commented. And so did the performers. 98° were just starting to hit it really big, after bubbling under for a while. Their album *98° And Rising* was on the charts, and the girls loved them. Everywhere they went, the shows were sold out. And with B*Witched being possibly even better known and well-loved, it made for a great atmosphere each and every night. The audiences sang along with "C'est La Vie," and loved the Irish dancing.

From Salt Lake City, it was east to Chicago, followed by a couple of dates in Ohio (Dayton and Cleveland), before hitting Detroit, where a completely bizarre event occurred. The rest of the girls were in the hotel lobby waiting for Sinead (she was probably putting on her lipstick). When she emerged from the elevator, a middle-aged woman dashed up and asked for her autograph. Quite happily, Sinead signed a piece of paper for her. But after looking at it, the woman seemed disappointed. Evidently, the woman had mistaken Sinead for Ellen DeGeneres, the comedian and star of *Ellen*, who'd caused such a controversy by coming out of the closet as a lesbian. Quite how the mistake had been made was baffling to Sinead—not to mention the rest of the lasses. There wasn't even a superficial resemblance between the two. But it gave them something to laugh about on the way to the show. At least the next two days were quite light in terms of travel, only having to go to East Lansing, then Grand Rapids. Then it was time for a mad dash to the East Coast, starting in New York, followed by Camden, New Jersey; Westbury, Wallingford, and heading into Pennsylvania for concerts in Pittsburgh and Wilkes-Barre.

By that point both bands were beginning to feel the strain. Singing virtually every night, even with amplification, was taking its toll on everyone's voices. They gargled, drank honey tea, and did everything they could to protect their singing. And there was also the sheer exhaustion of being on the road, day in and day out. Some of the time they did get to sleep in real hotel beds, but even then, in their dreams, they seemed to be moving. And most of the time it was a case of trying to sleep on the bus as the vehicle traveled at sixty miles an hour along the freeway. They'd wake up not knowing what state they were in or what time it was. It became a totally disorienting life. The only thing that was real was the road.

Down to Fairfax, Virginia, and Richmond, before heading back for a final swing into the Midwest and South. There was Columbus, Nashville, Atlanta, Charlotte, Louisville, Indianapolis, and finally, on May 8, Kansas City, Missouri.

It was just as well the two bands got along well; life would have been awful otherwise. Actually, they didn't see that much of each other. They traveled on separate buses, and most of their contact was at the shows, so it was only for a couple of hours each day. They were all too tired to even think about partying, although the girls weren't really into that, anyway. As April turned to May, they were all counting down the days until it would be over.

It had been great fun, but they all desperately needed a rest. Their voices were rough, their feet hurt from dancing so much (so it was probably just as well they always dressed in comfortable trainers!), and they felt like zombies—at least until they got out on stage and the screams started, the music kicked in, and they really came alive again.

Finally, though, it was all over, and now they could relax. There was, of course, an end-of-tour party for the bands and crew, who'd all found themselves working harder than they ever had in their lives, and had managed to sustain it all with good grace and great humor. Surprisingly, the girls wouldn't be leaving America straight away.

"We're [going] back on May fourteenth," Sinead said—and by back she meant Ireland and home, "which is my birthday—just get that in there! We're going back for nine days, and then we go to England for a few days to do more recording for our second album, then we're back in the U.S. basically for the rest of the summer."

So what would they do for six more days in America, apart from beginning to unwind in the Los Angeles sunshine? What would any girl do with plenty of money and time? They'd go shopping, of course, buying things for themselves and for their families and friends. Retail therapy was just what the doctor ordered after the last five weeks on the go. Charge cards in hand, they could spend part of each day hitting the stores, getting as wild as they liked, before returning to the hotel and just chilling by the pool. Finally, everything packed, it was time to head for LAX and board the flight to Shannon Airport in Ireland, where their families would be waiting to meet them and whisk them off for nine days of home-cooked meals and pampering. There'd be a chance to go out for drinks with friends, to catch up on all the gossip, and see all manner of relatives. With the relatively slow pace of life in Ireland, their bodies could finally slow down and return to normal.

By now, every trip home seemed like a luxury, and this was the last opportunity they'd have until September, at the very earliest. All the girls were close to their families, keeping in touch was important to them—particularly Keavy, with her massive phone bills. Actually having the free time to spend with them was becoming rarer and rarer, however. It was like heaven to eat a chicken stew made by their mums, to just sit and watch the television in the rooms where they'd grown up, and go to sleep in the beds where they'd slept as children. It was comforting, like being wrapped in a warm quilt. There was plenty of good Irish milk to drink, as much as they wanted, a chance to walk around, rather than spend their waking hours on a bus, and lots of fresh air.

Mostly, though, it was just rest and recuperation. For Edele, in particular, that meant resting her voice, which had taken a beating on the American tour. But, with the album now platinum, she knew it had all been worthwhile. They'd cracked the States wide open. "C'est La Vie" had slipped off the charts, but that was bound to happen. The next single would appear in June, to happily coincide with their next tour.

Of course, it couldn't *all* be rest. That would simply be too much to expect. There were tapes to listen to, of songs for the next album, and some rehearsals to be undertaken, as well as lyrics to be learned. Enough to keep them ticking over. And they were able to sleep as late as they liked. This time their parents wouldn't be dragging them from their beds to go to school or to work. They'd earned every second of rest that they managed to get. But nine days, as they discovered, wasn't a very long time. Certainly not long enough to completely overcome the exhaustion. Before they knew it, they were back at the airport for the short flight to London.

It felt weird to be in the Surrey house again. They hadn't been there since before the end of March, and now May was more than half over. Even though the landlord's mum had looked after it, there was still a mustiness and unlived-in smell about it. Luckily, with lots of great weather, they were able to open the windows and air the house out a little. All the sunshine and warm temperatures, though, made it harder to get back to work. When it was so beautiful that you wanted to just sun yourself in the back garden or go to the beach, who wanted to be cooped up in a stuffy recording studio?

Well, the girls did. They were eager to complete work on their new album, and it was very much a race. They only had three weeks in which to complete everything. After that they'd be on the road, a continent away, and anything that wasn't fixed would have to stay broken. Apart from anything else, these sessions would produce the next single, which the label wanted to release during the summer. B*Witched weren't even going to wonder yet if they could make it five in a row. Until the recording was finished, that really didn't matter.

Ray Hedges had worked his magic on the tracks. Working with his partner, Martin Brannigan, all the backings had been arranged and recorded. Without the special B*Witched quality, though, they were just empty instrumentals. The girls would make them sparkle and shine and come alive. That was what they did best.

The fact that they had a hand in writing much of the material on this album (as they had on the first one) belied any rumors about all pop bands being manufactured, and put together simply to get hits. In some cases that might be true, but not for B*Witched. They were a real band, the genuine article. True, they'd had incredible luck, but they'd also been working very, very hard to complete their success.

Now it was down to a lot of long hours, singing the same lines over and over and over, in search of that perfect take, to keep it all alive. Being a pop star might have looked glamorous to an outsider or a fan, but the reality was much more boring. Long hours in the studio, long hours on tour buses, never enough sleep. The glitter rubbed off pretty quickly when you started living the life. You had to be extremely dedicated to keep going.

Sinead, Lindsay, Edele, and Keavy were all extremely dedicated. That was why they were willing to push themselves so hard. It had all started as a laugh, but they'd quickly turned into real professionals. After so much time on the road, there was almost a telepathic communication between them now. They knew when to come in to help each other out vocally, what would work, what wouldn't. It truly was like magic. And with so much work to be done in such a short time, that was probably just as well. Back in the Sixties, entire pop songs had been recorded in three hours. Now it wasn't uncommon to take a week or two on a single track, sometimes longer. The girls were falling somewhere between the two. They might be killing themselves to meet the deadline, but it would sound absolutely perfect. Anything less and what was the point?

It wasn't just the recording, of course. There were a million other details to be taken care of: the upcoming American tour, cover art for the new album and single, video concepts, even bits and pieces concerning their British tour in November; there wasn't a minute's peace until they all fell into bed at night.

It was almost a relief when the eleventh of June came. By then they'd done all they could, polished and re-polished every single vocal track, added harmonies, backgrounds, and done everything that was asked of them, as well as a few things that hadn't been. Their voices were in great shape, protected in the studio environment. That was good; they were going to need them, given that they had more than two months on the road ahead of them.

Saturday should have been relaxing. Instead, it became shopping madness, going into London to stock up on things they'd need to take to America with them, since there'd be precious little time to shop over there, including, Sinead said, "Bras and knickers! Have to wear then every day. Need that clean underwear."

For once they weren't about to trust Sinead with the tickets, only to reach Heathrow Airport and discover she'd left them at home. No chances this time. They only had a couple of days' rehearsal before this tour began, and everything had to go right the first time.

The girls had signed on to be a part of the *All That* Music and More Festival. It was summer, and time for the big festivals to hit the road in America, like the Vans Warped Tour. This, however, was aimed at a different, younger audience, hence its association with the Nickelodeon comedy show that aired Saturday nights (and which had spawned *Keenan & Kel*). For anyone who thought you couldn't put together a major tour of pop artists, this was living proof that you could. There were seven artists on the bill, a couple up and coming, but most very firmly established: No Authority, Aaron Carter, Tatyana Ali, 3rd Storee, Monica, 98°, and B*Witched. That made for a pretty humongous bill, a lot of talent sharing the same stage. Of course, for the girls and 98°, it was like old home week—they'd only parted company just over a month before. They were used to each other, laughing and joking like buds. But it was a tour where no one could stand on ceremony or ego. Things had to move too smoothly for any of that.

To the girls, it was going to almost seem like picking up where they'd left off. In May, the next-to-last date on their tour had been in Indianapolis. Now this new tour began there, on June 17, a kind of freaky case of déjà vu. It was summer in the Midwest, hot, humid, and sticky—not the best weather to be wearing heavy denim and moving around a lot. If there was one consolation, it was that they didn't have to be up on stage too long each night. But it was still the best way to lose weight that any of the girls had come up with yet—dance it off in sweat. And the dressing rooms and buses were all air-conditioned, so there was some relief once they were finished.

Since this was a tour aimed at kids, there would also be time to talk to the fans, and sign autographs. That was why they'd paid their money, as much as to see the artists perform. That closeness gave a real sense of intimacy, something everyone wanted, rather than the big divide between singer and fan.

Their last tour had seemed carefully organized, but the girls hadn't seen anything compared to this. With so many acts, everything had to be timed to the minute; it was the only way for it all to work. There was a mass of equipment, as well as the tour buses, a convoy heading along the freeways of America through the night and the days. With a total of forty dates, it wouldn't be *quite* as grueling as their last trek around America; but it wouldn't be a picnic, either. When they'd toured with 'N Sync earlier in the year, the lasses had seen how cold some parts of America could get in the winter; now they'd have the chance to experience real heat, more than anything they'd ever known. With the *All That* tour going all around the country, they'd see the real differences in climate that America had.

From Indianapolis on June 17, it was off to Milwaukee the next day, followed in very quick succession by Cleveland and Detroit (hopefully no one would mistake Sinead for Ellen in Detroit again—that would be all she'd need!). From there it was a rush ride to the East Coast, to perform in Scranton, Pennsylvania, on the twenty-second. Then down to the ocean, and Virginia Beach straight after. It wasn't even an overnight stay, though, as they had in be in Nashville on the twenty-fifth, then St. Louis and Columbus, before heading up to Boston. If you followed it on a map, it looked crazy, and it was.

But that was the concert business. A lot depended on

exactly when a venue was available, and whether it could fit into the tour schedule. So, all too often, tours found themselves zig-zagging all over the place, even retracing their footsteps in part. It was nuts, but somehow it managed to work, although it tended to add several thousand miles of driving to each tour.

After Boston, it was down to Camden, back up to Rochester, then south to Charlotte, a detour to Pittsburgh and Hartford, then plunging down to Florida in July to dates in Tampa and West Palm Beach, with lots of bottles of water on the stage. Then came a long swing across the southern half of the States. Raleigh on July 13, Atlanta, Houston, Dallas, San Antonio, San Diego, Phoenix, and Irvine, before finally being able to catch their breath with a two-night stand in Universal City, California, (essentially Los Angeles) on July 26 and 27.

The main thing to fight in all of this was boredom and burnout. B*Witched loved performing—they were playing in front of audiences long before they made a record—but living for those few minutes on the stage every night was difficult. They made it all worthwhile, but you had to go through a lot to reach them. The endless traveling, a mixture of fast food and restaurants (although the girls did travel with their own cook, who made some of their meals; that definitely helped), sleeping on the bus or in an unfamiliar hotel bed that might or might not be comfortable. No real chance for sightseeing. The cities all became something of a blur, really, with little to distinguish them from each other, no chance to see what kind of character they might have.

The biggest factor was burnout, though. A single American tour could be exhausting. By the time this one finished, on August 21, the girls would have done *three* huge U.S. tours in eight and a half months. Many bands had broken up from the strain of doing less. And it wasn't as if they'd simply had time to recover in between. The rest of their datebooks were full too, as they would be after this. Once they got home, it would be time to promote the new single, then the new album. There was no rest for the wicked, even if they weren't in the least bit wicked. Still, this was what they'd dreamed of doing, and now it was a total reality.

From L.A., the *All That* tour would move north up the West Coast. First they'd play Oakland, then San Francisco, Sacramento, Portland, and Boise, before a date in Seattle (actually at The Gorge, some three hours east of Seattle in eastern Washington). Then, finally, they'd be on the final leg, slowly moving east again. August 10 would see them in Denver, the twelfth in Kansas city, the fourteenth in Cincinnati, the fifteenth in Rosemont, the seventeenth in Wantaugh, and then Holmdel, New York, closing three days later in Manassas, Virginia. There had been bigger tours, and longer tours, but this was massive enough, the type of thing it would be impossible to forget.

Of course, once it was over, the girls would take a few days in Ireland, and probably spend most of it sleeping or eating good, home-cooked food. The rest would seem very precious. But it would be far too short. What they really needed was a whole month off, with nothing to do but lounge around, catch up on the soaps, and sleep whenever they wanted.

There would be new photo shoots to be done, interviews, television appearances—and more traveling. Although they'd spent quite a while concentrating on America, the rest of the world still loved them, and wanted to see them. With a new album on the way, and a new single hot off the presses, there was no shortage of demand for public appearances. What were four girls to do? Oblige, that was the answer. At least they'd be adding to their frequent-flyer tally, even if they had no chance to cash them in for a real vacation.

The focus for the fall, and well into the winter, would be their second album, and the label was keeping very secretive about what it would be like—as were the girls themselves. The first indication would come when their British single appeared, not before, but to say it was eagerly awaited was putting it very mildly indeed. While BSB were tearing up the charts with *Millennium*, the girls were planning their own Irish invasion of the Top Twenty for the year 2000. Probably the only certainty was that there'd be an Irish strain running though it all; after all, that was their trademark, and as global as they'd become, there was no forgetting that they were an Irish group.

Most likely it would be the same eclectic mix as before. Some hip-hop, some ballads, some dance music, and some rock. They still loved all kinds of music, and, as Edele loved to say, they didn't like limits. With four top singles in Britain, they could pretty much do what they wanted in terms of music, anyway.

To some they'll always be the Irish Spice Girls, no matter what they do, no matter what they've achieved on their own terms. But they've come far enough not to let tags like that worry them any more—not that they ever did. By the time the Spices get around to releasing their album, they may even be thought of as the English B*Witched (okay, okay, it's not going to happen, but . . .). Right now they're like a fine-tuned machine, just racing along in top gear, and overtaking most everything else on the road. And there are no signs of them slowing down; they appear to have endless energy. From studio to tour, to tour to studio, they just keep on winning fans. And it couldn't happen to four nicer girls. What you see is what you get. And what you get, if you look or listen, is bewitched. But you already know that. The spell has been cast.

Conclusion

IT'S BEEN A WILD RIDE. Actually, it couldn't have got any wilder. In two years, the girls of B*Witched have gone from being nobodies to becoming major stars all around the world. If that's not a whirlwind, then nothing is. To say they conjured up a lot of magic when they got together has to be true—there's no other way to properly explain the way they've risen! How else can you go from just getting together to opening a national tour for a major band in a matter of weeks—with a spot on national television en route?

"Every day is a high for us," Lindsay said. "We wake up and go, 'Yay, we can't wait for work today!' "

If it all seems hard to believe for an onlooker, imagine what it must have been like for the girls, literally whisked away to stardom. Of course, there was a lot of work before the real stardom began, but they gladly put all that in, as they still do. In fact, they work much harder now than they did at the beginning. There's no chance of them ever taking success for granted, not that they ever would, anyway.

"I think you've got too much of something when you start taking it for granted," Lindsay agreed. "I hope I never get like that."

She hasn't; none of them have. It would be difficult to think of yourself as someone special when you've spent the last ten hours on a bus going along the American freeways, really. Yes, they're pop stars in what is really the first golden age of pop in more than twenty-five years, but more than that, they're four very hard-working girls who had a dream and saw it all become real. They're honest enough to be astounded by their level of success, and always have been.

"When I heard we'd got to Number One with 'C'est La Vie,' I thought it was all a joke," Edele laughed. "When

I realized it was true I started crying, I couldn't believe all our hard work had paid off."

These girls don't believe the world owes them anything. They're eager to keep working, to earn their successes—and those successes just keep on coming. The girls, though, remain exactly the same, happy to scamper home to Dublin when they have the chance, and sit around at their parents' the way they did when they were fourteen or fifteen.

"I thought fame might change me as a person, but it hasn't, not even slightly," Edele observed. "It made us excited for a while and we were proud that we had achieved what we set out to do but it really didn't change us."

There's no exotic lifestyles of the famous and rich for them. It's still the house in Surrey, and walking to the Laundromat to dry their clothes. Difficult to get an attitude when you have a bag of wet laundry on your shoulder!

Of course, there will be changes in the future. When they moved into the house in Surrey, they were unknowns, hoping for the big time. Now, although they still get along so well, there are times each of them could use some space to be alone. So it's quite possible that in the not-too-distant future we could see each of them moving into apartments (why would they need entire houses? They're never there, anyway). And it's hard to have much of a personal life when you're sharing a place with three other girls. While dating hasn't been high on anyone's agenda, rumors have bubbled up that Lindsay has been seeing Lee from Brit boy band 911, and you never know what else is going to happen.

One thing that won't change is that B*Witched will remain the top priority for all the girls. It's their joy, their fulfillment, their pride. And they all want to see exactly how far they can take it. Their friendship is stronger than ever, and if it can stand being cooped up together on three long, demanding American tours, it can endure anything! It's highly unlikely that anyone will be leaving for a solo career, at least not in the near future. They understand that there are absolutely no guarantees in this business, and that they could fall out of favor, but they handle even that possibility—remote as it is—with extreme maturity.

"Even if it all ended tomorrow, I'd be happy," explained Linds. "I just take each day as it comes and am thankful for what we've achieved."

But she should also be very proud of what they've achieved. That record of four Number One singles in Britain is unprecedented. They're working hard to make America theirs, and the country has been quite happy to come to them.

The reality is that they've only just started. The girls have a long career ahead of them. They haven't even released their second album yet. Of course, there's a lot of speculation about what it will be like, and whether it can top the first. But B*Witched really just served to establish them. They're barely out of first gear. If anything, they've been very cautious about the speed at which they've moved. Most bands who've done what these four girls have done wouldn't be content to be a support act on an American tour; they'd be demanding first-class treatment and a headlining slot. But taking it slow can pay a lot of dividends in the long run. It means they get to know more people, and establish a stronger rapport with audiences. No one here is about to wig out and become a diva.

Being down-to-earth is the only way they know. When Sinead goes home, her mum still sends her out to do the shopping. And when Edele can honestly say that her favorite piece of clothing isn't some expensive designer dress but "a pair of jeans that are frayed around the edges" (for Keavy it's her baggy Levi's) then you know you're not dealing with a bunch of egos and prima donnas.

Even more, they can laugh at themselves, the accidents and embarrassing moments they've had, onstage and off. They love what they do, but they don't take themselves too seriously. They're not precious about things. It's a very healthy attitude.

In time, almost undoubtedly, all four of them will settle down and marry. That day remains a long way off, however. And even after it comes, there's absolutely no reason why they can't continue making music as a band. Even now, they cross a lot of age barriers in their appeal. While it's primarily to teens, you can also find plenty of mums and dads buying and playing their records, and who also think they're great. To be able to catch so many people is a rare feat indeed, and says a great deal about the girls themselves, and the breadth of their own tastes that they've worked into their music.

Pop will never go out of style. It comes and goes, stronger at some times than others, but it never completely vanishes, unlike so many of the fads (can you say grunge?). A good pop band can go on for a long time. But it's only in the last few years that girl groups have really broken through, and of those, only the Spice Girls and B*Witched have really stood out. But whereas the Spices have chosen to fly high after establishing themselves—and they truly did appear with a bang!—B*Witched have continually offered a much more human face. Will the two have equal longevity? All the Spices are now incredibly rich young women. B*Witched are, too, even if it's not to the same extent. But they seem to have more of a work ethic about them, a commitment to the music more than to the fame.

Of course things will change in the future. Who would want them to stay still? The girls will grow, both individually and together. Their image might well change, away from denim (as in the video for "Blame It on the Weatherman") and into something more adult. Whatever alters on the surface, though, the heart will still be exactly the same—some things *don't* change.

Life for the girls is good, if somewhat demanding. They remain every bit as sparkly as their name, or as the B*Witched rings they had made. They're four individuals who came together to forge some magic, and they've more than managed that. Perhaps as much as they're grateful to their fans, the fans should be grateful to them, for releasing so much great music, and being willing to tour so much in support of it. Watch a B*Witched show, whether it's the first or the fortieth on a tour, and you can see that they're having fun, enjoying every second of entertaining people.

"A lot of people have said that when they watch us on stage they can't get up off their seats because they're afraid they're going to miss something excellent," Edele noted, and you can't get much higher praise than that. At the same time, a lot of people *do* get up and dance. So the girls end up with the very best of both worlds. It's easy to see why fans adore them—they give one hundred and ten percent, every time.

Could B*Witched be one of the bands for the new millennium? Why not? They're young enough, and they have enough talent to keep themselves going well into the next century. And they've paced themselves well enough to take advantage of it. This November will see their very first headlining dates, on a British tour. They've been in no hurry to make the transition to headliners, although it's been one of their goals. And they have a lot of plans for those shows. According to Keavy, "You'll walk in and you'll know you're at a B*Witched concert. That's all we're gonna say!" Sounds very intriguing!

There's no sense of calculation about these lasses. While they think ahead, as you have to, it doesn't seem to be all about "career moves" and stuff like that, the way some bands seem to plan it all out. But when you're not a manufactured band, when you're doing it for the sheer joy of doing it, you can afford that luxury.

They know how lucky they've been so far. There have been very few dues that they've had to pay, really, since their ascent has been so rapid. But, while that's true, it's helped them keep a freshness about things, and make it seem as if everything is an adventure—which, for the most part it still is (although those American tours have become a bit grinding). Let's face it, very few bands get plucked from obscurity on their first public performance—of course, very few bands make their live debut on national television.

They opened with a splash, and they've kept it that way. Like a lot of bands nowadays, B*Witched have an official web site (not to mention all the unofficial fan sites in cyberspace), which just won a CADS award for Best Artist site. On top of that, from 948 entries, theirs was voted best site in the Dotmusic Readers' Choice Awards—a pretty high honor. But it just seems as if they can barely put a foot wrong. About the only thing they haven't won lately (at least, something for which they've been nominated) is an Ivor Novello Award, given in Britain for songwriting. Robbie Williams, the former leader of Take That whose solo career seems to be finally taking off in the States, walked away with a couple, and most of the rest went to the songwriters who penned Cher's comeback, "Believe."

Still, as the girls would definitely point out, it's not about awards—it's about pleasing the fans. And fans love them. Which might be why "C'est La Vie" is set to appear on the British version of the CD *Songs From Dawson's Creek*, although they're not to be found on the U.S. version of the compilation. Quite why there'd be a different track listing for different countries is one of life's little mysteries.

Beyond a new album and their November tour, what can we expect from B*Witched? Well, a lot more music, for a start, although not all at once. Over the years, though, there'll be a number of albums and singles. And they need to re-establish themselves in other parts of the globe, after spending so much of 1999 concentrating on America, so tours of Europe and Asia are very likely.

One thing no one should anticipate is a B*Witched version of *Spiceworld*, the movie. The girls might make videos, but that doesn't mean they have any great inclination toward acting. Music is quite enough to satisfy them. And don't be too astonished if they decide to take a few months off in the not-too-distant future. They've certainly earned a break after all they've done in the last couple of years. At least three months, possibly as long as six months, although by that time they'd certainly be chafing at the bit to get back to work, since it seems to energize them more than anything!

Although no dates for it have been included on their British tour, it would be unthinkable for them not to play some show in Ireland. They've always celebrated their Irish heritage, and it was Irish television that gave them their big break. So it's possible that over Christmas or Millennium Eve they might do a few concerts (although Millennium Eve would likely have been announced by now) in the Emerald Isle, leading into a vacation there.

And will they ignore America for a while, having spent so much time there? Yes and no. There won't be any tours there before the year 2000, that much is for certain. But they've worked so hard to establish a fan base that perhaps they won't need to tour for a while. No matter where in the country their fans live, there has been an opportunity to see them perform. Rather than just letting the videos play on MTV, or relying on the Disney Channel concert special, they've truly gone out of their way to take themselves to their fans. They've made a long, concerted effort, and that's important. It's possible that they might tour again—as headliners this time—early in 2000, since their next album is unlikely to be released in the U.S. before then. But that would depend on a lot of factors.

"I believe the things that happen to you happen for a reason," said Keavy, and the things that have happened to B*Witched have all occurred because of the music they make. They communicate joy. They love what they do—singing and dancing. They're four everyday girls who got together and found a little bit of magic. "We're the same as our fans, it's the secret of our success!" laughed Sinead, and it's perfectly true. Any girl can relate to B*Witched. The clothes are the same, the hair is the same. They're casual, but together they sparkle. It's not just chemistry, it's alchemy, really, and if someone could bottle what these lasses have, they'd make a fortune!

They are, as Lindsay points out, "thankful for what we've achieved." It's exceeded every expectation they ever had. Even Keavy and Edele, who'd seen their brother Shane hit the big time, have been overwhelmed by the way things have happened; B*Witched have certainly eclipsed Boyzone internationally. And they've done it on their own, through their own talents and hard work. It's not, as Linds pointed out, "about glamour, 'cause what we do isn't really glamorous at all, it's hard work." And it goes to show that even in a corporate, prefabricated world, there's room for talent and originality.

While it's not completely a rags to riches tale, there is a lot in the B*Witched story to inspire anyone who's dreamed of making the big time. It really is possible. The fabulous four might say they're not feminists themselves, but they're still role models to a new generation. And just doing what they do makes them feminists. They're helping to break the mold, they're more than stereotypes. In and of itself, that's an inspiration. As a band, they're not about limits, as Edele has stressed, and that means in every way, not just musically. They've shown that they can really dance, really sing, really write, and tour just as much as any of the boys (even more so, in fact). So it doesn't go under the phrase "Girl Power?" Who cares what you call it, or if you call it anything—it exists.

B*Witched have given people what they wanted, and they've done it on their own terms, by mixing it all up and coming out with something familiar but fresh. And by just being themselves, polite, full of the gab, and very Irish. It's impossible not to like them, so there was never any point in trying to fight it. The world was ready for them, even if it didn't know it yet, and the band popped on the scene. Right time, right place, right talent, some luck. A perfect fit. And perfect fits happen rarely. When they come along, you stick with them. The B, the cat, the shamrock, and the star—it's proved to be a very potent combination indeed. It works, and no one's knocking that. Some perfect pop for now people. And that's what the world needs—and it always will. It's what B*Witched have to offer. To you. And you. And you.

Just don't expect them to go away anytime soon. That's the thing about magic—it has a tendency to stick around.

Discography

Singles
U.K.

C'est La Vie/ We Four Girls/ B*Witched Quiz Show
Rollercoaster/ Get Happy
To You I Belong/ Fly Away/ B*Witched's Message to Santa
Blame It on the Weatherman/ Together We'll Be Fine/ Blame It on the Weatherman (Orchestral Version)

Album
U.K.

B*Witched
Let's Go (The B*Witched Jig)/ C'est La Vie/ Rev It Up/ To You I Belong/ Rollercoaster/ Blame It on the Weatherman/ We Four Girls/ Castles in the Air/ Freak Out/ Like the Rose/ Never Giving Up/ Oh Mr. Postman

Singles
U.S.

C'est La Vie/ Get Happy/ B*Witched Quiz Show/

Snippets from We Four Girls/ Rollercoaster/ To You I Belong

Album
U.S.

B*Witched
Let's Go (The B*Witched Jig)/ C'est La Vie/ Rev It Up/ To You I Belong/ Rollercoaster/ Blame It on the Weatherman/ We Four Girls/ Castles in the Air/ Freak Out/ Like the Rose/ Never Giving Up/ Oh Mr. Postman

On The Web

So you've got your modem roaring at 56K, and you're after B*Witched stuff. Sure you could go to a search engine. But why not save yourself the time and use this handy guide instead?

The best place to begin is with the official site, *www.b-bwitched.com*, which has some good info and interviews, pictures, and a schedule for the girls, as well as notes on other things. A very cool, very handy place to start. There's also the Epic Records site, *www.epicrecords.com/b-witched*, where you learn more from the American angle.

Official sites are great, but it's when you get to fan sites than you meet the real obsessives. And—surprise!—there are lots of B*Witched fan sites, all wonderfully unofficial, and lots of them pretty amazing. There's also a B*Witched Webring. In that you can click from one site to the next very easily. The B*Witched Headquarters Webring Site is at *www.geocities.com/Hollywood/Location/7811/b-witched.html*.

Rik's B*Witched site can be found at *members.xoom.com/riksbwitched*, so now you know. A cool Scandinavian site is B*Witched Online (*w1.303.telia.com/~u30303181/*).

B*Witched@1 Hyper Place has a lot to offer, and you can avoid gridlock by surfing directly to *locket.net/1hyperplace/bwitched/*.

Do also check out the very sweet site, The Color In My Life—*www.angelfire.com/mi2/TheColorInMyLife*.

Sidz B*Witched on the Web even has a chatroom where you can meet other fans, which is a great idea: *bwitch.cjb.net*.

These are far from the sum total of B*Witched sites. But if you follow the links, then you'll probably eventually hit them all. Good luck.

GET THE SIZZLING INSIDE STORY ON THE WORLD'S HOTTEST BAND!

BACKSTREET BOYS

They've Got it Goin' On!

Anna Louise Golden

Find out all about AJ, Brian, Howie, Kevin, and Nick step into their world, see what makes them tick, what kind of girls they like, how they make their way-cool music, and much, much more! Includes eight pages of cool color photos.

BACKSTREET BOYS
Anna Louise Golden
0-312-96853-1_____ $3.99 U.S. _____ $4.99 CAN.

Publishers Book and Audio Mailing Service
P.O. Box 070059, Staten Island, NY 10307
Please send me the book(s) I have checked above. I am enclosing $_____ (please add $1.50 for the first book, and $.50 for each additional book to cover postage and handling. Send check or money order only—no CODs) or charge my VISA, MASTERCARD, DISCOVER or AMERICAN EXPRESS card.

Card Number_____
Expiration date_____Signature_____
Name_____
Address_____
City_____State/Zip _____
Please allow six weeks for delivery. Prices subject to change without notice. Payment in U.S. funds only. New York residents add applicable sales tax.

BOYS 10/98

Meet Hollywood's Coolest Young Superstar!

MATT DAMON

By Kathleen Tracy

Matt Damon is more than just a handsome heartthrob—he's also a talented actor and screenwriter who took home both a Golden Globe Award and an Oscar for co-writing the movie *Good Will Hunting*. Find out how he made it in Hollywood, what he plans for the future, about his lifelong friendship with Ben Affleck, about his steamy relationships with some of his leading ladies, and much, much more! Includes eight pages of exciting photos.

MATT DAMON
Kathleen Tracy
0-312-96857-4 _____ $4.99 U.S. _____ $6.50 CAN.

Publishers Book and Audio Mailing Service
P.O. Box 070059, Staten Island, NY 10307
Please send me the book(s) I have checked above. I am enclosing $_____ (please add $1.50 for the first book, and $.50 for each additional book to cover postage and handling. Send check or money order only—no CODs) or charge my VISA, MASTERCARD, DISCOVER or AMERICAN EXPRESS card.

Card Number_____
Expiration date_____Signature_____
Name_____
Address_____
City_____State/Zip _____
Please allow six weeks for delivery. Prices subject to change without notice. Payment in U.S. funds only. New York residents add applicable sales tax.

DAMON 10/98

**THE QUEEN OF HIP-HOP,
THE CROWN PRINCESS OF SOUL,
AND THE VOICE OF A NEW GENERATION.**

LAURYN HILL
She's Got That Thing

CHRIS NICKSON

In her amazing solo work, and as part of the Fugees, Grammy winner Lauryn Hill creates music that is both spiritual and political, entertaining and educating—soulful, original, and real. Her solo album, *The Miseducation of Lauryn Hill*, was the fastest-selling debut ever by a female artist. Her storybook romance with Bob Marley's son Rohan, father of her two children, along with her phenomenal music and her blossoming acting career, make for a well-rounded, successful life at any age—and Lauryn's just starting out! Read her fascinating story and educate yourself on what it takes to achieve greatness—on your own terms.

WITH EIGHT PAGES OF COOL PHOTOS!

LAURYN HILL
Chris Nickson
0-312-97210-5___$5.99 U.S.___$7.99 Can.

Publishers Book and Audio Mailing Service
P.O. Box 070059, Staten Island, NY 10307
Please send me the book(s) I have checked above. I am enclosing $_____ (please add $1.50 for the first book, and $.50 for each additional book to cover postage and handling. Send check or money order only—no CODs) or charge my VISA, MASTERCARD, DISCOVER or AMERICAN EXPRESS card.

Card Number_____
Expiration date_____Signature_____
Name_____
Address_____
City_____State/Zip_____
Please allow six weeks for delivery. Prices subject to change without notice. Payment in U.S. funds only. New York residents add applicable sales tax.   LH 3/99

Get the sizzling inside story on the hot young star of song and screen

SITTIN' ON TOP OF THE WORLD
ANNA LOUISE GOLDEN

Named one of the "21 hottest stars under 21" by *Teen People* magazine, Brandy, the chart-topping singer and star of TV's *Moesha*, is one of today's hottest young talents—a bright, headstrong woman who handles the hurdles of stardom with major maturity, while enjoying life like an ordinary teenager (she talks for hours on the phone, shops up a storm, and *loves* McDonald's french fries!). Get the 411 on this award-winning superstar and her life in front of the camera, in back of the microphone—and *behind* the scenes.

WITH EIGHT PAGES OF FABULOUS PHOTOS!

BRANDY
Anna Louise Golden
0-312-97055-2___$4.99 U.S.___$6.50 Can.

Publishers Book and Audio Mailing Service
P.O. Box 070059, Staten Island, NY 10307
Please send me the book(s) I have checked above. I am enclosing $_____ (please add $1.50 for the first book, and $.50 for each additional book to cover postage and handling. Send check or money order only—no CODs) or charge my VISA, MASTERCARD, DISCOVER or AMERICAN EXPRESS card.

Card Number_____
Expiration date_____Signature_____
Name_____
Address_____
City_____State/Zip _____

Please allow six weeks for delivery. Prices subject to change without notice. Payment in U.S. funds only. New York residents add applicable sales tax.   BRANDY 3/99